Environmental & Natural Resource Management

Environmental & Natural Resource Management

H.K. Mishra

FORWARD BOOKS
New Delhi • Guwahati • Visakhapatnam

FORWARD BOOKS
4649-B/21, Ansari Road
Darya Ganj, New Delhi - 110 002
Ph.: 23263193 / 9811582579 / 09435116718
Fax: 011-23263193
Email: ektabooks@yahoo.com
www.akanshapublishinghouse.com

Environmental & Natural Resource Management

First Published 2011
ISBN 978-81-909742-9-5

PRINTED IN INDIA

Published by Forward Books, New Delhi and Printed at Harmain Offset Press, Delhi.

Contents

Preface

> "The trouble with average budget is that it's hard to fill up one hole without digging another."
>
> —*Dan Bennett*

The nature has bestowed our earth planet with abundant natural resources and a clean environment and ecological system which are ideal to lead a healthy life. It is apt to mention here that all natural resources are limited, only some of which are renewable. Increasing population pressure and materialistic greed of human beings have abused, misused and overused the natural resources; resultantly our environment is badly affected and polluted to such an extent that survival of any life on earth is at stake. Atmosphere, biosphere, hydrosphere, fauna and flora all are threatened.

As a healthy environment is necessary for survival of all life on the earth, the current deterioration in it has attracted the attention of all thinking people from all over the world.

In fact, environmental economics is concerned with the impact of the economy on the environment, the significance of the environment to the economy, and the appropriate way of regulatings economic activity so that balance is achieved among environmental, economic and other social goals. The very process of producing certain commodity for meeting the demands of consumers is bound to create/produce certain products-gases, wastes etc., which are not environmental friendly. Thus, essence of environmental problem is the economy-producer behaviour and consumer desires. In the absence of the economy, most environmental issue remains simply research questions of concern to chemists or biologists with no policy significance.

Today, in a modern complex economy, one relies on markets to match producer costs with consumers demands to yield the "right" amount of pollution (and thus consumption), for most goods and services. The basic problem with pollution is that markets do not work to produce the socially desirable amount of pollution. This shows the breadth of the problem which needs to be corrected. However, this poses several questions: What is the incentive behind the generation of pollution? What is the cost and societal gains from pollution control? What regulatory mechanisms can be designed to ensure the right balance between costs and gains? Sometimes these issues are straightforward, other times they are very complex.

Assessing the economic value of the environment is a major topic within the field. Use and indirect use are tangible benefits accruing from natural resources or ecosystem services. Non-use values include existence, option, and bequest values. For example, some people may value the existence of a diverse set of species, regardless of the effect of the loss of a species on ecosystem services. The existence of these species may have an option value, as there may be possibility of using it for some human purpose (certain plants may be researched for drugs). Individuals may value the ability to leave a pristine environment to their children.

In this present book we have taken the theme—environmental and natural resource management. All pertinent issues are suitably addressed. The following chapters make core of study—Concept of Environmental Economics; Economics of Natural Resource Management;

Environmental Demand Theory; Macroeconomic Policies and Environment; Ronald Coase's Theorem of Property Rights; Effects of Environmental Regulations on Economy; Hedonic Value Method; Environmental Accounting; Environmental Tariff; Environmental Audits; Conclusion; Appendix and Bibliography etc.

Definitely, this will serve the purpose of one and all concerned.

As the theme is well documented by different scholars in the field, we have liberally borrowed their expert opinions to furnish the authoritative information. I express my deep sense of gratitude to them all. I am equally grateful to all sources of information which I have made use of. Though I have tried to acknowledge them in references and bibliography, if any name is left that is unintentional. My teachers, colleagues, friends and family members have been instrumental in my academic performance, I am deeply beholden to them also. I cannot miss to mention the cooperation and inspiration of my wife and kids who provided congenial work environment at home. Finally, I am thankful to my publishers for materialising this effort elegantly in the present shape.

—H.K. Mishra

1

Concept of Environmental Economics

> **"Mental tension is supplanting muscular fatigue as the chief complaint of workers in newly automated fac-tories, according to a recent study by Yale University. New machines have eliminated drudgery but the strain of watching and controlling them is said to make workers "jumpy." Jobs are physically easier, but the worker now takes home worries instead of an aching back."**
>
> —*Homer Bigart*

Economics is a basic social science emcompassing study of all aspects of life, e.g., from birth to death. It is both theoretical as well as applied.

As a healthy environment is necessary for survival of all life on the earth planet, hence emerged the field of economics of environment and natural resources management.

Since our prime focus in this work is on economics of environmental and natural resources management, first let us have a look at environmental economics.

First it is pertinent to note that the environment as per *Encyclopaedia Britannica,* "is the complex of physical, chemical and biotic factors that act upon an organism or an ecological community and ultimately determine its formed and survival. Thus, the environment is the system in which human being has to adjust to the natural as well as economic, social cultural, political and legal situations/factors, for its habitation and survivals.

All these factors affect the environment and are also affected by the environment. Similarly, environment and economics have kith and kin relationship so much so that there is a common belief that economics is the root of the "environmental problem."

However, environmental economics is concerned with the impact of the economy on the environment, the significance of the environment to the economy, and the appropriate way of regulatings economic activity so that balance is achieved among environmental, economic and other social goals. The very process of producing certain commodity for meeting the demands of consumers is bound to create/produce certain products-gases, wastes etc., which are not environmental friendly. Thus, essence of environmental problem is the economy-producer behaviour and consumer desires. In the absence of the economy, most environmental issue remains simply research questions of concern to chemists or biologists with no policy significance.

Today, in a modern complex economy, one relies on markets to match producer costs with consumers demands to yield the "right" amount of pollution (and thus consumption), for most goods and services. The basic problem with pollution is that markets do not work to produce the socially desirable amount of pollution. This shows the breadth of the problem which needs to be corrected. However, this poses several questions: What is the incentive behind the generation of pollution? What is the cost and societal gains from pollution control? What regulatory mechanisms can be designed to ensure the right balance between costs and gains? Sometimes these issues are straightforward, other times they are very complex.

It is significant to note that the environmental economics for the first time emerged from the "think tank" Resources for the future in 1950s and got momentum from 1970s. In 1950s Ford Foundation, set up an Environmental and Resource Economics Research Organisation as Resources for the future (Rff) at Wshington D.C., to address problems of material shortages. Clawson and Knetsch, 1966, Alan Kneese, Kneese and Bower, 1968, Krutilla, 1967 and many others worked in this field. The 1990s payoff is taken as the beginning of the influence of the environmental policy, marketable permits for pollution control are today widely embraced, valuation methods have become integral part of environmental prevention, wide application of environmental valuation in decision-making concerning major public projects with environmental impacts, and in environmental economics has become major key role determinant in the current climate change debate.

As such, after having a view at the historical development of environmental economics, it is pertinent to study its various dimensions in more detail. In the following description we shall first discuss the relationship between environmental economics and environmental policy and then its relationships with economics, ecological economics, resource economics, etc. finally, we will consider several important issues, currently the subject of much research and debate, that confront the field of environmental economies. In the last the concept of various environmental goods is given an elaborate treatment.

Environmental Economics and Environmental Policy

The increasing pressure on the earth due to rapid growth population resulting in high density of population and wreckless increase in wealth in the worlds has aggravated the concern of the environmentalists all over the world. Not only this, high population density in most of the world threatens the earth's automatic of absorbing and cleansing capacity of human and industrial wastes. Income is also important, not only because wealthy people tend to consume more and thus generate more pollution, but also because the environment is often viewed as a luxury good. The environmental issues, occupy for the poor people, comes in the last (sometimes even not considered) after the other pressing needs related to survival.

As people become wealthier, they become more conscious about the quality of their living environment, which ultimately is planet. Thus, one can confidently believe that the world will be more concerned in future towards environment, if the present trends of increasing wealth continues. This may be of varying dimensions in different countries of the globe.

In fact, developed countries, preservation of natural environments (e.g., wilderness areas) and pollution are major concerns. Pollution problems usually involves two major issues—(i) knowledge of right quantity of pollution and (ii) the polluters control their emissions.

(i) What is Right Amount of Pollution?

It must be remembered that it is not easy to determine the right amount of pollution, as it is generated as a by product of producing goods. For obtaining the costs of pollution control, it is imperative to understand the process of production of goods and various levels of casts for different level of pollution. However, a producer can apply any or may technique is to reduce the pollution, besides investings in research and development to find new ways of controlling pollution.

Similarly, consumer has the option of reducing the consumption of polluting goods. Thus, it is easy to conceptualise the costs but is very tedious to measure it empirically. This comes under the domain of environmental economics. The determination of right amount of pollution also involves determining damages form pollution. The pollution affects both flora and fauna and it is not easy to evaluate the damages caused by pollution, especially in the case of damage to health. (i.e., itching eyes, reduced visibility, decreased lung capacity, tensions and worries about the adverse effects, increased susceptibility to illness, and of course illness itself).

Some people believe that it is a natural science question, which is nothing but oversimplification of the multitude of ways pollution affects people and the relative seriousness of these effects to the people. However, economics is accustomed to condensing this variety of effects into a single measure—the willingness to pay to reduce pollution. People are ready to pay (use resources) to reduce get rid of bad pollution.

Barring the option that polluter should pay, our way of measuring the overall magnitude or importance of pollution reduction to a person is through his/her willingness to giveup something valuable in exchange for improved personal environmental quality. Measurement of this willingness to pay is not an easy task and is the subject of much research in environmental economics.

Further, once the individual's willingness to pay is determined, it is possible to add up individual preferences to obtain a societal willingness to pay to reduce pollution. It is then easy to combine this with the cost of pollution control to determine the socially optimal amount of pollution reduction. But, how to obtain this is the biggest question. One way is that government may provide incentives and undertake research to reduce costs for the future pollution regulation.

So, providing/formulating a well-accepted pollution control policy, is the prime challenge before environmental economics. This problem, though has been discussed in the case of developed economies, does applies to developing countries too. The same issues of costs, demand for clean-up, are in developing economies also.

A clear-cut definition/description relating to preservation of natural environment, is another significant policy question. This could involve protecting animal and plant species form vanishing (extinction) or preserving wild life and scenic vistas (areas) form development. Here, the basic problem is providing balance between the forces of development that threaten these environmental resources and the social value of preservation. The quantification of both sides of the equation, when they are confronted with very specific decisions, to help policy makers, is the biggest problem.

As environmental protection involves the intervention of government in the economy and it is often difficult to decide on the proper extent and nature of that intervention. The environmental economics, as it is applied to real environmental problems can be invaluable in helping make those important decisions.

Environmental Economics and Economics

As we all know economics is a well-developed discipline with an extensive body of theory, a praradigm associated with how the economic world works, and a number of branches, or fields of study, associated with pieces of the economy.

Basically, the theory of consumer, the theory of firm, and the theory of market interaction which forms the basis of nearly all of economics, are the subject matter of micro-economies. Not only this econometrics and other applied economics are also included in micro-economics. Labour economics, health economics, monetary economics, developmental economics, experimental economics, international finance, law and economics and environmental economics etc. are included in microeconomics. For the most part, each of the these fields has helped in some way understand the economics beyond its narrow set of interests. For example, Labour economics helped in many innovations in econometrics which has been applied across economics.

It is apt to mention that microeconomics theory has many branches which has contributed in various ways to market to the over all study of economics, besides being concerned with major portions of economic activity. Some of them worth mentioning are: macroeconomics (the study of aggregate as opposed to individual phenomena), public finance (the study of goods not provided by the market and the study of taxation), individual organisation (the indepth study of how firms interact with each other and with consumers and organise themselves into industries), and international trade, etc.

Remarkably, like other branches of economics, environmental economics has also enriched the methods in the area of nonmarket valuation, i.e., methods for measuring demand curves for goods when there is no market. Not only this, environmental economics has successfully adopted various tools developed in other streams of economics to questions regarding the environment.

Apparently, environmental economics is an applied field like many other applied fields of economics. It has also adopted various concepts developed in other branches of economics (particularly public finance and industrial organisation) in solving environmental problems are unique to the field (such as valuation) and have potential use in economics outside of the field of environmental economics.

Environmental Economics and Ecological Economics

It must be remembered that "environmental economics" and "ecological economics" belongs to two different perspectives, but their ultimate objectives are to help make social decisions about environmental problems. In this respect some people do not make any difference and treat "environmental" and "ecological" word synonymous to each other.

Basically, in environmental economics, economists are involved to apply their discipline and paradigm (models) to consider the environment, while in ecological economics, ecologists are involved to use their discipline and paradigm to consider humans and the economy. This is one fundamental distinction between the two disciplines. The other distinction is related to the modus operandi, i.e., how these two fields approach environmental problems.

It must be remembered that ceological economics is made of two words—*ecology* and *economics*. The word ecology, derived from the Greek word 'oikos' meaning habitation, and 'logos' meaning discourse or study, implies a study of the habitation of organism. Ecology has been vividly defined as 'scientific natural history' not the study of biotic communities,' or 'the science or community population,' or, 'a study of animal and plants in their relations to each other and to their environment (surroundings).

In other words it is a scientific discipline that studies the interaction between organisms (Plants animals, bacteria, virus, mycoplasma)' and the environment in which they live. Ecology treats its subject matter similarly by a combination of empirical observations, educational reasoning and understanding the behaviour of the system.

Noted ecological economist Robert Costanza defines

ecological economics "as a "field of study that addresses the relationships between ecosystems and economic systems in the broadest sense." Here, the emphasis is on the very long-term health of the ecosystem, broadly defined (i.e., with humans as part of it).

In fact, the broad distinction between the two subjects lies in the measures of value of the environment. The general (conventional) economists believe that the value to society derives from the individual values held by human members of society. On the other hand ecological economists take a more bio-physical view of value for instance, some ecological economists measure value in terms embodied energy contents. Thus, in comparing a type writer to a computer, the appropriate question is which took less energy to create? Less energy is better.

This is a direct extension of ecological theories that ecosystems operate to minimise the through put of energy. However, for derivation of a public policy should base on the energy contents of delivered goods and services. But environmental economists do not agree with the proposed "energy theory of value" given by ecological economists. It is erroneous to consider only one factor, i.e. "energy content," and leave several other factors like labour, land etc., which do work as resources in short supply. It is nothing but an oversimplification. For environmental economists, the value of a good stems from its embodied content of multiple scarce factors (including energy) as well as how much value individual people place on the final good. In other words, value cannot be reduced to a simple physical metric.

It is pertinent to note that distinction between the two fields is very apparent when one considers the environmental problems with very long-time horizon, such as disposal of nuclear wastes or global warming. Environmental economists has no hesitation in admitting that it is difficult to analyse the problems in which costs and benefits spread over long period. For instance, if one wants to analyse the cost and benefits of storing nuclear wastes for a quarter of million years. This will involve potential risk.

Here, the benefits of the storage taken/enjoyed by the present consumers of nuclear power, while costs, if any, are borne by future generations that must live with the nuclear repositories. In this case, traditional economists will add all of the costs and benefits and will apply a discount factor to reduce the importance of future costs in the total. This implies that todays decisions are least affected by the future's happenings. This may be disquieting to many of us. Recent atomic reactor disaster in Fukushima (Japan) has made this question clear.

However, ecological economists will opt the notion of sustainability approach to deal with the inter-temporal problem of decision. For them, any action not sustainable in long run will prove disadvantageous. In the above example of nuclear waste, they would be anxious to know: ?Whether we can continuc to bury waste forever and ever and be satisfied with the world that results? The negative reply means that action is not sustainable. It does not relate to equilibrium of costs and benefits in any way. There is some intuitive appeals to such a philosophy. Here, we are concerned with static (short term) issues only. Questions of long-run tradeoffs and dynamics are the purview of resource economics.

Environmental Economics and Resource Economics

Generally the field of environmental economics and resource economics are put together in our envelope, because both concern the natural world. In environmental economics we are concerned with excessive production of pollution by market or insufficient protection of the natural world, due to market failure. On the other hand, resource economics is concerned with the production and use of both renewable and exhaustible natural resources like fisheries and forests. Nonrenewable resources would include minerals and energy as well as natural assets such as the Himalayas and species of plants and animals (fauna and flora).

Though, these two fields of study differ from each other, even then they overlap. Environmental economics is concerned with static questions of resource allocation. The decision related to right amount of vehicle emmissions in New Delhi does not involve/depends time issue. On the contrary, it is time factor which makes renewable and exhaustible resource question interestings (an area of resource economics). It concerns with dynamics. For example, if we cut out forest slowly over a long period the forest will regenerate and we can continue the process indefinitely. The scarcity in future of the exhaustible resources and its price will depend on the rate/speed of extraction of these resources market failure, her, is not the essence of problems in both the cases.

The Global warming, climate change, preservation of natural environments, etc., are some example of overlaps between environmental and resource economics. These issues involve time so they could be linked with resource economics. On the contrary, damage to natural environments is often the outcome of economic activity with a different result of conversion of habitate to human use. Perhaps the most distinguishing division between environmental and resource economics is between static issues related to natural world and dynamic issues.

Nature of Environmental Economics

Obviously, for an economics graduate it is not difficult to differentiate between the positive and normative perspectives. In positive economics, one tries to explain what we see in the economy around us. It is more value free. Its aim lies in providing explanations about the evolvement and working of markets and institutions.

In normative economics, one tries to explain how we would wish the economy to allocate and distribute goods and services. It tries to apply economic tools to design government policies to intervene in the marketplace. What world be the "best level" of intervention, become the basic question. Clearly, this requires a way of defining what is best—a much more value-laden process than merely explaining why the economy works as it does.

Like conventional economics, environmental economics is both positive as well as normative in nature. One can not remain restricted to positive economic while working with environmental problems. The notion of market failure is the fundamental to environmental economics. The correction /repairing of the market failure requires intervention of government. What kind and levels of intervention? This is a normative question. Here the role of environmental economists becomes imperative. They have to formulate the normative theory, involving value-judgement, to correct market failures or the public provision of non-market goods.

Environmental Economic Issues

It is significant to note that measuring the demand for non-market goods has been most important to economies. This has become central to many public debates over environmental quality. Some of these methods, viz., stated preference methods, contingent method, etc., has invited attentions of both critics and supporters. Some people feels that these methods are valid and of tremendous significance. While some people takes it as best biased and worst vacuous. However, a very active area of current research is the theory underlying methods of measuring the demand for environmental goods as well as empirical methods for doing so.

Another point of contention revolves around the regulation of environmental goods. It is essential to refine the economic incentives before they can be relied on to solve many real environmental problems. These difficulties are related to incentives, different amounts of information possessed by polluters and the government, and the role of technological change in determining future levels of pollution control.

Another problem is related to understandings, the environmental regulations interact with trade restrictions (or lack there of). The compatibility of differential environmental regulations with free trade, exploitation of environments of developing countries by free trade etc. are also major issues in environmental economics. These are certain areas which need proper investigations and research.

From the foregoing description, it can safely be surmised that economics of environment is of much relevance in the present day complex environment, where ecological balance and environmental health is regularly deteriorating and life is at the verge of extinction.

Nature is supreme, it is sacred and it must be protected and used in sustainable way. Though nation-states and world organisations have framed many laws and enactments for conservation of environment yet much is to be done. Modern economic activities and corporates have a social responsibility in this direction and efforts are being made for environmental auditing and reporting.

In the subsequent chapter we will put light on

environmental and natural resources management economics.

REFERENCE

Costanza, R., (ed.), *Ecological Economics: The Service and Management of Sustainability,* California University. Press, N.Y. 1991).

2

Economics of Natural Resource Management

"Every individual has a place to fill in the world, and is important in some respect, whether he chooses to be so or not."

—*Nathaniel Hawthorne*

The nature has bestowed the universe and more specifically our planet with abundant natural resources. The earth (soil), air, water, forests, minerals, fauna and flora and everything on this can be termed as natural resources. These are used and reused for various economic activities (purposes) by man.

As the human population increased rapidly the limited natural resources were being exploited indiscriminately—better say abused and misused. No consideration was given for scientific use of these and no preservation and regeneration (of which could be) measures were adopted. It is only when man directly felt the consequences of overexploitation of natural resources in the form of epidemics, droughts, famines, acid rains, landslides, global warming and climate change, need for a proper natural resource management was felt.

In this chapter we will introduce you to main natural resources, threats thereto and conservation methods.

The sum of all physical, chemical, biological and social factors which compose the surroundings of an object referred to as environment and each element of these surroundings constitutes a resource on which plants and animals including men draws in order to develop a better life. Thus any part of our natural environment such as land, water, air, minerals forest rangeland wildlife fish or even human population that can be utilizes to promote welfare of living being may be regarded as a natural resource.

In fact, a resource can be defined as a form of energy and or matter which is essential for the functioning of organisms, populations and ecosystems In the particular case of humans a resource, is any form of energy or matter essential for the fulfilment of physiological, social, economic and cultural needs both at the individual level and that of the community.

The functioning of ecosystem of technological civilization involves a continuous flow and consumption of energy sun being the source of its as regards ecosystem and fuels as regards technological civilization. In the light to this fact a resource maybe defined as one of the various forms of primary energy, which present in the nature.

It is apt to mention that five basic ecological variables energy, matter, space, time and diversity are sometime combinedly called natural resource. As such laws which govern changes in these quantities have great applicability in the resource use.

Classification

Basically, resource can be classified in two categories: (a) renewable and (b) non-renewable.

(i) Renewable Resource

The renewable natural resources are those which are reproducible and are obtained from the biomass of living organisms e.g. forests and fish. Solar energy although having a finite life as a special case is considered as a renewable resource inasmuch as solar "stock' are inexhaustible on the human scale.

(b) Non-renewable Resource

The resource which are not reproducible and are obtained from the finite non-living reserves are called non-renewable resources e.g. coal and metals some authors prefer to classify resources into biotic (or living) and abiotic (or non-living) resources, forest, agriculture, fish and wildlife falling in the first category and land water minerals etc. in the second.

CHART 1

Classification of National Resources

Natural Resources	
Inexhaustible	***Exhaustible***
Unlimited or unending. Quality may be degraded not quantity.	Limited both qualitative and quantitative degradation possible.
Immutable	***Mutable***
Quality not degraded by men's activity e.g., atomic energy, wind power, precipitation, tidal power,	Quality may be degraded by men's activity, e.g solar radiation, water, hydropower of running waters.
Maintainable	***Nonmaintainable***
Availability depends upon method of use by man.	Total Quantity state, when consumptively used, not replaced.
Renewable	***Nonrenewable***
Perpetual harvest possible, e.g. fertility of soil, bio-products of land, fresh water and sea, human power.	Once gone, on replacement e.g. species of wildlife,
Reusable	***Nonreusable***
Consumptive use small e.g., gems. nonconsumptively used metals like gold, platinum, silver, iron, copper, zinc, ingalvanized iron, tin in tooth paste	Consumptive use high, e.g., fossil, fuel nonmetallic minerals like gypsum, sand, salt; consumptively used metals like lead in gasoline and paints, zinc containers.

Natural Resources: Conservation and Management

Etymologically, the term conservation is derived from two Latin words—cont—together and *servare* to keep or guard. The dictionary meaning of the word is an act of preservation'. Thus, the conservation is a practic embracing preservation, maintenance, sustainable utilization, restoration and enhancement of the natural environment. Summarily the true aim of conservation is twofold: First preservation of quality of environment, and second to ensure continuous yield of useful material—living or non-living—by establishing a balanced cycle of harvest and renewal.

It has been an established fact that total natural resources available are limited, the wayout to the problem seems only through control of population and also the per capita consumption of resources. Because it is difficult to bring down per capita consumption, the recycling and stringent conservation can bring hope for sustained development without reducing per capita use of resources.

Now let us have a look at the presence, and management of various national resources, viz., land, water, forest, rangeland, wildlife minerals and energy, etc.

Land

Soil consists of the weathered layer of the earth's crust with living organisms and products of their decay intermingled. Lying on the rocky core of the earth, this complex mixture is one of the four prime requisites for life Alone with sunlight, air and water, soil supports all living beings on land plants as well as animals. All higher terrestrial plants have their roots in soil from which they absorb life sustaining water and nutrients. Man and all land animals, in turn depend on these plants for food directly or in directly. Foods, vegetable oils and fats, forage for livestock, fibre wood and various other indispensable agricultural products come from soil. Thus a nation's economic well being is inextricably linked with the fertility and abundance of soil resources.

Productive land is since the source of human sustenance and security everywhere at all time, this resource because of mounting demands of swelling population and long mismanagement would put in jeopardy the very survival of man.

Land Use and Abuse

The land although appears to be resource available unlimited but, in fact, its injudicious use would limit the availability of this indispensable life-support system. Thus, a land use may be poor or good. If in a region of low rainfall grasslands are replaced by wheat crops, a temporary desert will eventually result; or if the human habitation and factories are developed on flood plains the damage is almost inevitable. These are the instances of poor land use. Conversely, if the grasslands are used for moderate graizing by livestock and if the flood plains are used for forestry or agriculture, these will imply good land use. Ecological principles have great applicability in land use planning. Classification of use should, therefore, be based on natural ecological features of the land in question, viz, soil type, slope, biotic communities etc.

Planning of Land Use

(a) Rural Land-Use Planning

In rural land-use planning, concentration is chiefly devoted to creating and developing more farmland by removing forests and natural grasslands, draining marshes and swamps, channeling streams for irrigation and so on. Unfortunately no effort is made to save existing prime farmland from degradation by ill-planned development. Rather than exclusive farm, range, or forestry oriented planning, the land use should be made under broad consideration of social, economic, and ecological intricacies.

(b) Urban Land-Use Planning

A planned cities are as necessary as planned farms. Although the implementation of land-use plans is infinitely more difficult in urban areas than in rural ones because of the human problems involved yet if not needed it would lead to chronic pollution epidermics and social disorder.

In any urban land-use planning it should be seen that;

(1) at least a third of all land remains as protective open space in the form of parks green belts, or refuges etc, including adequate space for efficient treatment of domestic and industrial wastes;

(2) residential housing around villages or cities should be developed in clusters with each unit separated by broad green belts;

(3) typical topographic situations like stream valleys, steep slopes, lakes and marshes, etc. Should be retained free from houses and other high-density uses; and

(4) waste disposal areas and industries should be kept apart from human habitations.

Land Management

Obviously, from the above account it is clear that major problems emerging out of abuse of land in cities include unsafe and out of abuse of land unhygienic dwellings and those in rural areas are of erosion of soil and loss of fertility While urban problems can be prevented and cured by proper town planning and municipal facilities while the problems relating to rural areas need long terms soil conservation programme.

(a) Soil Erosion Prevention and Control

The primary purpose of soil conservation is to prevent soil erosion and health damage where it has not advanced too far to respond to curative methods. This is possible largely through two means.

(i) The land should wear a vegetational cover throughout the year. Plant roots bind the topsoil and prevent it from being drifted so easily with water or air. The vegetative cover also slows up runoff water and causes much of it to percolate into ground that romotes more vegetative growth. The vegetation-whether grasses, these, or cultivated crops-should fit to the capabilities of the soil and water available.

(ii) Engineering and agronomic practices should be applied cojointly to counteract the erosive force of both water and wind on the soil. These include contour cultivation, cover crops and crop rotation, and contour strip-cropping, uses alone or in combination.

(b) Reclamation of Eroded Lands

Conservationists are divided into two camps over the issue of reclamation of land already arrested by ravines. One camp of Conservationists and naturalists believes in the policy of forgive and forget and advocates that ravines should be allowed to exist, while the other fells that efforts should be made to regain the lost land through building or some other means. If the ravines are left in there present state, these will spread further and engulf more of productive and while the violent means to regain to ravines in their near original condition may provoke numerous agencies of nature to take revange on man.

Thus, following considerations are important in negotiation the eroded land:

(i) Ravines should be provided with sufficient and suitable vegetative cover.

(ii) Instead of agriculture, these lands should be reclaimed for forestry, pasture, or horticulture.

(iii) Their deficiency in nutrients and moisture for plant growth should be improved.

(iv) Further misuse of such land should be prevented. Over-trempling by man and cattle should be avoided.

(v) Past damages should be repaired and recompensed under strict ecological consideration. For instance depressions may be filled up, slopes easened out, cattle trails fenced etc.

(vi) Vegetative cover provided should be protected against reckless destruction by local population.

WATER

It is believed that the volatile constituents bound in the earth's crust, oozing the surface through volcanose, rock movements, and hot springs, condensed to form the ocean and the atmosphere. This way perhaps this remarkable combinous of hydrogen and oxygen-called water-came into being and eventually become an indispensable component of the earth's environment. Water moves from the ocean to air to land to ocean in a set cyclic pattern called *hydrologic cycle*. In other words, this cycle represents a continuous process of exchange of water from the earth's surface to the atmosphere and vice-versa under the influence of solar heat.

According to an estimate of the total available water 97.3 per cent is contained in the oceans and out of remaining

2.7 per cent most is in solid form. The amount of water actually available in the atmosphere is a very minutes faction and estimated to be only 1 10^{-5} of the world's total water.

In fact, factors which control the process of evaporation and evapotranspiration include temperature, humidity and wind. It is a continuous process going on dry and night from the ocean surface, ground surface, inland waters (like lakes and streams), plant and animal surfaces. Rising in the atmosphere this water form clouds that flood around in gaseous or droplet form. The atmosphere above the earth up to varying heights of 10 to 17 km (depending upon latitude and season) is called the *troposphere* up to which the clonus float and in which all weather changes take place.

Water returns to the earth in the form of precipitation, most of which takes place over the ocean and a little on the land surface. Rainfall on the land surface may have following fatest it may percolate through the soil and become a part of ground water regime, accumulate in a pond, lake or reservoir as inland surface water flow down to the ocean in the form of stream, taken up by plants and animals, or evaporate.

Requirements and Uses

Goether rightly said that everything originated in the water, and everything is sustained by water. Water is needed to fulfill diverse requirements in so many divers ways. It is vital to life since for all physiological activities of plants and animals it is essential. On an average it institute 80 per cent of protoplasm ranging from 8 per cent in dry dormant seeds to 95 per cent in jelly fish.

It serves not only to quench the thirst but also to meet the food requirements, because it is an essential raw material in the process of photosynthesis through which green plants make food that is used by all trophic levels directly or indirectly. Ambients humidity which is indeed the invisible form of water that surrounds us in necessary to prevent dessication of terrestrial life forms. Thus, it can be said that water is a biological essential. Flood plains of rivers have been the cradle of civilization and centres of population since ancient times. The reason being their high fertility and easy accessibility to water for various uses like drinking, washing and transport. Egypt was developed on the flood plains of the Nile, Babylon on the Tigris, and North India on the flood plains of the Ganges. Even today the Mississippi plain is about the most densely populated area in the USA as flood plains of the Rhine in Europe, and the Yellow river in China. Besides temperature, water is the other such key factor that influences the global ecology. Covering about 70 per cent of land surface and circulating in hydrologic cycle water influences water and climate of any region and thus, its flora and fauna.

In fact, agriculture is dependent on water may it be rainfall or surface or ground water irrigation. It eventually is a more important commodity in a country like India because her largely agrarian economy depends critically on water. Huge amount of protein rich food in the form of fish shell fish and prawn is obtained from the inland as well as sea waters world over. Aquaculture has come up as a very potent industry. The kinetic energy of gravitational flow of water is tapped and transformed into electricity what is called hydropower. This concept of electricity generation is one of the oldest and cheapest tricks largely used worldover.

Moreover, it leaves on pollution burdon on nature as in case of thermal or nuclear power generation. Hardly any industry can do without water. It has multifarious application in industrial processes viz, a raw material solvent chemical reactant coolent and cleaning agent.

Water everywhere not any drop to drink is the situation not only found amidst sea but also at places where industrial and domestic refuse make the benevolent water sources so severely contaminate with pathogens and or toxins that they are left unpotable. Being the best dilution medium it is frequently used as the cheapest and convenient way for liquid and solid waste disposal.

Further, it was practical impossible to maintain sanitary conditions without water for it is needed in all common cleanings and washing practices. Water at many places serves as a very convenient means of navigation. Besides, it adds to the aesthetic value of the landscape and provides opportunities for recreation and sport. Water being undervenly distributed over the land influences interstate and international relations and thus is the cause of what is known as hydro-politics. It can therefore be said that while water is an essential for life it is significantly linked with social economic political and ecological intricacies.

Water Management

Management of water implies making the best use available water resources or human benefit while not only preventing and controlling its depletion and degradation but also developing it in view of the present and future needs. Water, like forest is a multipurpose resource and it is important to see that its various uses should not conflict with each other and it can be enjoyed in its totality by man and others.

Thus, its right allocation, and quantitative and qualitative conservation are the primary tasks before water managers. Floods, droughts, improper use, pollution, and disease transmission are the important problems related to water. Because usable inland water resources constitute a very minute fraction of the world's total water and because man largely depends upon this minute fraction of water for his various activities. It is important to make efficient use of available water and at the same time prevent abuse of it.

This has to be considered not only in giant irritation projects or industrial and municipal processes but also in very day life. Taps running unpurpose fully, leaking water supply pipes, using filtered water for gardens and building construction are a few instance of inefficient and misuse of water in daily life-Water being the best and convenient dilution medium is worst affected resource by pollution.

To a common man pollution of water means only the drainage of industrial effluents or domestic sewage in natural waters. It may astonish a lay reader that even pure distilled water when released in sea may act as a pollutant since it alters the normal salinity of sea water, which adversely affect the marine life. Besides, chemical alterations, changes in physical condition of water also have grave effects on the biota of system as during thermal pollution caused by the discharge of heated effluents in a body of water. Pathogens, chiefly entering natural waters through municipal wastes rich in excreta and other organic filth, also render the water unsuitable for human use.

It must be remembered that, it is not only the man who has to use the water resources but these are equally important to land, animals and more to those fish and other aquatic animals who live in it. Thus pollution of a body of water does prove detrimental not only to the human society but also to regional ecology and the ecology of wary aquatic ecosystem.

It is therefore, essential that the water should not be

treated as a simple repository of water disposal and if inevitable the waters only after proper treatment should be released in it under strict ecological consideration. The qualitative degradation of water is also in a way quantitative depletion of usable resource. Therefore, recycling of waste water after due treatment would relieve the water scarcity to a great extent, especially in regions marred by water shortage.

The demand for potable water, like any other resource, is increasing fast with the rapidly increasing world population and continuous increase in per capita demand linked with more of sewage disposal and transport prolific use of water using gadgest (like air cooling and conditioning devices, washing machines etc), and increased recreation activities. According to an estimate the daily per capita demand for water of an American was 600 gallons in 1900 which increased to 1,500 gallons in 1960 and was 2,700 gallons by 2000. The situation is not different in developing world. Thus, the question is where will the water needed for fulfilling increasing demands come from? The answer is not so simple and can only be found through long-term planning. Possible means of meeting out the impending water deficit problem include: (i) reclamation of sewage and waste water; (ii) development of ground water sources and surface storages; (iii) long range forecasting of rain (iv) rain making; (v) transfer of surplus water; (vi) desalination of sea water; and water harvesting on modern lines.

FORESTS

In common parlance, by forestry we mean natural ecosystem having multispecies and multi-aged trees as dominant community. Forests cover about one-third of the earth's land surface of which about 50 per cent is occupied by tropical forests. Of the total geographic area of India, 22.74 per cent is forest as against a minimum of 33 per cent forest cover prescribed under National Forest Policy.

Forests are necessary for protection of natural environment and also for sustainable development.

Major Functions

In fact, functions of a forest may broadly be classified into following three categories:

(a) *Protective Functions:* These include the protective role of forests against soil erosion, droughts, floods, intense radiation etc.

(b) *Productive functions:* Forests are the source of wood and many other products like gums, resins, fibres, medicines, honey, bidiwrappers, pulp, paper etc.

(c) *Accessory functions:* These include the role of forests in recreation, aesthetics and as habitat of diverse wildlife fauna and flora etc.

As such, it can be accepted that forests are important in two ways— ecologically and economically.

(a) Ecological Significance

From the perspective of environment, the forests are very important. They help in balancing oxygen and carbon dioxide level in atmosphere, regulate earth's temperature regime and hydrologic cycle. Forests increase local precipitation and water holding capacity of soil thus, preventing drought situation. Vegetational cover provided by forest impedes the velocity of runoff on soil surface thus checks soil erosion, silting, and landslides and reduce the danger of flood. The litter derived from fallen leaves maintains fertility of soil by returning the nutrients. Forests also act as refuge of wild animals and provide protection to them against strong, cold or hot and dry winds, solar radiation, rain and predators.

(b) Economic Significance

It is pertinent to note that wood, which has various applications in domestic and industrial processes, is the chief product of forest. Wood when used as fuel has certain advantages over coal as its sulpur and ash contents are very low but at the same time excessive use of fuel wood means pressure on forests which have many other functions to serve. Wood may also be converted into solid (coke), liquid, and gaseous fuels. Timber is an important material in construction and day-to-day uses.

Forest provides raw material for various wood based industries, viz, pulp, composite wood, rayon and other manmade fibres, sport goods, furniture, boat building, matches etc. Miscellaneous products like bamboos, resins, gums, some oils, fibres, medicines, katha, lac, shellac, etc., are also procured from forests.

Problem of Depletion

Increased urbanization, and mining has entailed indiscriminate felling of trees and denudation of forests. Nobody will, however, ever learn that who set the first assault on which tree in the history but this practice of logging down trees for human use has been going on for centuries unabated. Colonists used logs for fire-wood and making huts.

They also made handles for their tools, furniture, and fence posts etc., from it. For them forest had only a present and a past—no future; thus the resorted to ruthless and accelerated exploitation of available forest—a story that still continues with more serious backlashes earth has ever witnessed. India alone is losing more than 1.5 million hectare of forest cover each year and according to many workers.

25 million hectare of forests have been destroyed during the last three decades due to over exploitation and misuse and conversion to agricultural fields. The depleted forest wealth would simply deprive the man of economic and environmental values offered by forest, as discussed earlier

Forest Management

In forestry, the yield is chiefly obtained from the accumulated growth of the past, *so* this industry has to depend upon the annual growth. Forests are managed to obtain a sustained yield which is obviously possible through sustained growth.

Following considerations are important in this direction:

- A forest should have in correct proportion the trees of different ages and classes so that continuous removal of exploitable produce would not affect the future yield.
- Each tree crop should put on normal growth increments.
- No obstacle should exist to the continuous harvest of exploitable stems.
- Unrestrained felling should be prevented.

For all such planning and decision-making, sound ecological acknowledge is desirable that include knowledge about climatic conditions, composition of biotic community, successional trend, life cycle of important tree species, methods of arresting growth of undesirable trees and promoting growth of highyield tree species, and biotic interrelationships (such as weed. competitions, pests, parasites and diseases etc). Or various tactics employed in forest management, some deserving special considerations are as follows: (1) restrained felling, (ii) block and selective cutting, (iii) reforestation, (iv) control of disasters, and (v) recycling of forest products.

RANGELAND

A rangeland is the grassland that provides natural pasture for grazing animals. Grassland occur where rainfall is too low to support the forest community but is higher than that which results in desert community. Generally, in grassland precipitation ranges between 25 and 75 cm. However, depending upon edaphic factors, such as a high water table grasslands may also occur in regions of forest climates. Soil a grassland is characterized by having high humus content.

Over 6,000 species of grasses, adapted for a great variety of climatic regimes, cover about 20 per cent of the earth's surface. In size they vary from small plants as about 1 cm to over 35, tall bamboos.

Significance

In fact, man has been cultivating various grass species as his food and as fodder for his domesticated livestock since time immemorial. History of human civilization is the witness of dependence of man on the seeds of various grasses as his own food for instance, Indo-Chinese, American and Mediterranean cultures were based on rice, maize, and wheat respectively while forage was used as fodder for domesticated livestock. A range, if not serving as a direct source of food for man, still serves the making in a number of indirect ways. Solar energy transformed into food energy by the green cover of the range is available to primary consumers (grazers-domesticated or wild) as food, wherein a part of it is converted into meat.

Of considerable importance to man are these herbivores and their products, such as meat, milk, skins, hides, horns, and wool, etc. It can thus be said that at the root of all biological resources man utilizes is the forage.

Threat of Depletion and Degradation

Man would not destroy an artificial pasture developed by input of his hard labour and money than a natural pasture. Thus, like all natural resources, the rangeland, inflicted with human strees, is depleted and degraded. Causes of such stress may be ignorance green or incompetence of man. Phenomenal growth of cattle industry on one hand is responsible for ruthless over grazing, while on the other hand, wide expansion of urbanization, industrialization, and agriculture has resulted in encroachment of rangelands, compelling ranchers to overstock the available limited rangeland.

Often, out of green too a rancher allows a number of head to grazed beyond the carrying capacity of the range, being ignorant to the fact that too many sick and weak head would not fetch him as much value as *a* few head in prime condition of health after grazing on enough good forage. Community or ecological indicators provide the most practical approach of determining whether or not a range is being utilized properly (Humphrey, 1962). Range managers use the term decreaser for palatable species vulnerable to grazing; their disappearance is an indicator of grazing stress. When such indicators are not needed, unpalatable weeds invade and flourish.

Thus if overgrazing continues, decreasers keep on disappearing replaced by weeds. Once established it may become had to eradicate the weeds and not only this such vegetation will invite a variety of pest animals like rodents and insects. This makes clear the long-term consequence of overgrazing in range.

There is increasing need to restore the depleted and

degraded rangeland not only out of economic (livestock production) but also ecological consideration since rangeland depletion would also cause problems like soil erosion, spread of pests etc.

Range Management

In fact, the range management is defined as the science and art of planning and directing range use so as to obtain the maximum livestock production consistent with conversion of range resources. Efforts to manage a rangeland include regulation of grazing pressure, manipulation of stock (herd) distribution, burning of range, reseeding of rangeland, selection of cattle breeds, and control of weeds, pests and predators.

AGRICULTURE

The practice through which specific plant species are cared and managed so as to obtain maximum yield of consumable parts of the plants is called agriculture. An agricultural field is in fact a cropland ecosystem in which ecological principles involving limiting factors and productivity provide great applicability.

The demand for food production linked with tremendous population growth has been increasing fast world over. This has been possible to feed increasing number of mouths through increased agricultural production, what is called green revolution. It has resulted chiefly from the industrialization of agriculture. Which involves highly domestic plant species sophisticated chemical and large fuel energy subside. According to an estimate, to double the crop yield through industrialized agriculture a ten fold increase in fertilizers, pesticides and horsepower is required. The green revolution through industrialized agriculture as compared to conventional agriculture (man—and domesticated-animal powered) has following demerits:

(a) Such agriculture involving huge amounts of fuel and chemical in the form of fertilizers, pesticides and weedicides is the chief cause of environmental pollution.

(b) It may lead to social backlashes when a quick shift from small farms to large industrialized (corporate) farms takes place. In this process small farmers and agriculture workers are driven off the land to cities where they may not get work, food and housing a situation of despair and social breakdown.

In retrospect, strong measures should be taken to control the population growth, and to improve the conventional agricultural practices with application of current agricultural research under due social and environmental consideration.

Sustained Agricultural Production

- Available and acreage should be properly and judiciously utilized.
- Soil fertility should be increased through wise use of fertilizers and organic manures.
- High yielding and disease resistant plant varieties should be introduced.
- Mixed cropping should be practicised wherever possible.
- Integrated and balanced use of available water sources, surface and ground water, should be made.
- Weeds and pests should be efficiently controlled. Integrated pest control practices should be preferred over total reliance on chemical pesticides.
- Soil erosion and loss of nutrients should be prevented through maintaining vegetational cover throughout the year.
- Exotic varieties should only after due consideration of long-term impact be introduced.

WILDLIFE

Even on global level there appears and to be great deal of ambiguity attached to the term wildlife. Webster's dictionary defines wildlife as living things that are neither human nor domesticated specially mammals, birds and fish hunted by man. In American usage term 'wildline' is used to designate the game and excludes fish thus, they have fish and Wildlife Services at the federal level. In India too, the common understanding of the people regarding wildlife is of wild animals and shikar, more particularly mammals, birds, and reptiles. However, a report entitled Wild Life Conservation in India (1970) of the Indian Board of Wildlife states wildlife as the entire native uncultivated flora and fauna of the country. The wildlife (Protection) Act, 1972 also defines wildlife as any animals, bees, butterflies, Crustacea, fish and moth, and aquatic land vegetation which form part of any habitat.

Thus, a comprehensive definition of wildlife may be given as any or all non-cultivated and nondomesticated life including both, plants and animals.

Significance

The wildlife resources provide aesthetic recreational and economic benefits and at the same time are important ecologically. Nature's millions of forms of life on this earth performs some or the other definite biological function which keeps the delicate balance of our ecosphere. In nature flora and fauna go hand-in-hand and one cannot exist without the other. Birds and insects are necessary for the cross pollination of flowers, and these with other animals also serve for dispersal and propagation of vegetation. Not only this, the health of vegetation also depends on natural browsing and grazing. Needless to mention that animals directly or indirectly depends on green plants for their food. Besides food plant also provide shelter to a variety of animal species.

Equally important are the relations among animal populations. If too many herbivores are killed the predators deprived of their natural food will leave forest become wermin and pay upon domestics livestock of even man. On the other hand if too many carnivores are killed the herbivores because of release of predation pressure will become too numerous and acquire the status of pest for agricultural crops. Thus, most important is the balance of nature of which wildlife is an integral and important part.

Theats of Abuse and Depletion

One often comes across the headline in newspaper like 'Last of the blur whales' 'Save the golden langur' tragedy strikes sea turtles, 'Major downfall in rhino population', 'Great Indian bustard on the road of extinction' and so on, which arract the sad story of abuse and depletion of our wildlife heritage. According to an estimate, in last about 2,000 years the world has lost, by way of extinction, about 160 species of mammals and 88 species of birds.

It is pertinent to note that the India is endowed with a rich biological heritage and the various scriptures and epics are full of vivid and beautiful account of wildlife. Over 500 mammalian and 1,200 avian species contribute to the richness of this wealth. Unfortunately today the Indian wildlife, as that in many other parts of the world, is threatened because of man's unprecedented intervention with nature. Nearly 134 plant species have been declared threatened as against 71,47 and 15 species of mammals, birds and reptiles respectively. Great Indian bustard (*Choriotis nigriceps*) confined to the semi-arid regions of Rajasthan and Gujarat, and the white-winged wood duck (*Cairina scutalata*) inhabiting the Brahmputra swamps and the flood plains of Assam are both on the brinke of extinction.

Wildlife Management

Basically, conservation, is the practice embracing preservation, maintenance, sustainable utilization, restoration, and enhancement of the natural environment. Wildlife conservation in this sense is the management of nature's living resources if we consider wildlife as consisting both of wild flora and fauna. Since one cannot manage living resources while being indifferent to the non-living environment, the concept of wildlife management becomes the concept of management of natural ecosystems. It also overlaps forestry insofar as it is based on multiple landuse concept and implies management of wild plants as well as wild animal.

However, under the present dispensation wildlife management implies management of wild animals as distinct from forestry, and it implies maintenance of habitats suitable of the different species. In America and Europe wild animals, particularly mammals are treated as game crops, as do timber in forestry and food crops in agriculture and hunting is developed as a viable economic activity.

In America, wildlife and wildlife related recreation forms multimillion dollar industry. However, in India it is difficult to develop game as an industry because: (a) our forest areas are already overburdened with grazing pressure of domesticated livestock and because of already scarce pasture lands there is little hope of reducing grazing pressure in the forest areas to develop game, and (b) hunting as a source of recreation is beyond the means of the majority of population.

During past decades the wildlife management implied the understanding increasing and controlling of some species.

Sanctuaries and National Parks were mostly meant to protect a particular species or a group of species and to a limited extent for tourism and recreation. Today, however, the emphasis is shifting from the management of species to the management of ecosystem. The objectives of wildlife management, as outlined in the World Conservation Strategy, are thus as given below:

- To maintain essential ecological processes and life support systems in natural ecosystems, on which human survival and development depends. These essential ecological processes and life support systems can be defined to include maintenance of both the biotic and abiotic components of the ecosystem.
- To preserve genetic diversity (i.e., the range and variety of genetic material in the world's wild plants and animals) on which depend the breeding programmes necessary for the protection and improvement of cultivated plants and domesticated animals, as well as much scientific advance, technical innovation, and the security of the many industries that use living resources.
- To ensure the sustainable utilization of species and ecosystems. This will include the proper utilization of wild animals for game forest and grazing and to achieve proper integration for economy both of rural communities as well as trade and industry.

It is pertinent to note that people have been alerted now and the strong measures being taken in favour of restoring maintaining, and increasing wildlife population give hope that our rich legacy of wildlife will not only be saved for future but developed further.

Ways and means employed in wildlife conservation include:

(i) Protection of breeding stocks by enacting game laws and developing wildlife refuges;

(ii) artificial stocking including introduction of exotics,

(iii) control of predators;

(iv) habitat improvement; and

(v) game farming.

MINERALS

Basically, minerals are the nonliving substances obtained from the earth through the process of mining. Formation of minerals took place predominantly in weak zones like mountains, folder and faulted regions, lakes, and continental shelves through geological processes going on since billions of years.

Main Characteristics

Minerals possess certain peculiar characteristics, which distinguish them from other natural resources. These are:

(a) Exhaustibility: Minerals are non-renewable or depleting assets and one mined out the deposits get depleted and lost for ever without any chance or replenishment. Refuse of water, however, can be consumed afterwards though improved benefitication technology.

Simply this exhaustible resource cannot be cropped year after year like agricultural. Therefore three distinct stages can be identified in the life cycle of a mine: youth development stage; maturity-established stage; and old age-declining ore reserves. If the rate of mineral consumption is increasing fast, the knowledge about more reserves and potential substitutability of many minerals is also being improved. As such these predictions may prove outlined.

(b) Unpredictable Occurrence: The quantity and quality of a mineral in any region is not easy to predict. Uncertainties prevail with respect to their occurrence, extent of depth, cost of mining (often linked with depth), and the grade.

(c) Localised Occurrence: Minerals are very localised in their occurrence and the total areas occupied by them is far limited. Most of the mineral deposits are very apotadie in distribution, for instance. Kolar gold fields of India occupy an areas of 8 km by 1.6 km. Formations containing coal and petroleum are, in general bigger as compared to metalliferous deposits. The coal-bearing formations of India, for example, occupy about 4 per cent of the country's total area.

(d) Risk Involvement: The process of mining involves large number of problems for minerals. Abnormal temperature and pressure variations, rock burst, fire and gas hazards, lack of ventilation and drainage, collapse of roof and side walls are the peculiar problems encountered only in mining industry.

(e) International Character: Minerals know no political boundaries. Virtually, on country within its own boundaries has adequate production and reserves of all the minerals needed for its industrial development. The unequal distribution of minerals makes the international trade in its inevitable. Some countries are bestowed with monopolistic rights of certain minerals deposits with result in what is known as geopolitics.

(f) Dependence on Other Factors: Mineral production is largely affected by factors like the changing needs of consumer industries, availability of stock fluctuations in prices, and reuse of metallic scrap in production process. A technologically poor country possessing richer grades of ores may have to face keep competition in international market with technologically richer countries may however, possessing poorers grades of ores since in later case the cost of production is considerably low due to improved mining methods.

Development and Conservation Apprehension

Geologists are of general apprehension that the known reserves of minerals may not last for long and most of them will be exhausted within 100 to 200 years. New possibilities of mineral reserves in land and beyond the land as in the seabed are being explored which may reduce, if not totally remove the futuristic fears of exhaustion of the resource.

Presently, ilmenite, rutile, tin ore, diamond, sulphur, coal, petroleum, and calcareous and ferruginous seasands are largely being mined from the sea-coasts and sea-beds. In India ilmenite, rutile, and associated zircon, monazite, and sillimanite are obtained from beach sands of Chennai and Kerala coasts. Coral limestone for industrial use like manufacture of calcium carbide, and calcareous sand for cement are being mined from the sea-bed at Tamil Nadu and Dwarka (Gujarat) respectively for quite long time. Indonesia, Thailand, and Myanmar recover considerable tin ore from the sea-bed, while England recovers coal and Philippines iron from the sea-bed. A number of petroliferous structure occurring off the coast are being mined for petroleum and its products at several places. The ferromanganese nodules or what commonly known as manganese nodules found over the oceanic floors, generally below 4,000 m depth, are perhaps the most spectacular discovery in this field. The most prolific concentrations of such nodule with high metal values have been found in North pacific between 139° W to 141° W and 40° N to 16° N. Although precise information about the reserves of manganese nodules is not available but it is estimated that they may run several billion tons and may prove to be potent source of metals like manganese, nickel copper, and cobalt. It is estimated that 1 million/tons of manganese nodules from sea-bed provide about 275,000 tons of manganese, 13,000 tons of nickel, 1,2,500 ions of cobalt, and 1,000 tons of copper besides other metals like iron vanadium, molybdenum, silver and lead. Further, it has now been roughly estimated that the metal resources available in manganese nodules are several times greater than those available in land, such as cobalt 5,000 times, nickel 1,500 times, and copper 150 times.

Conserve Mineral Resources

- Application of efficient methods of mining to take out every possible tonnage lying ground.
- Utilization of unmarketable ores through the innovative methods or are dressing and metallurgical practices,
- Use and reuse of scraps
- Recovering all associated elements as co-product or by-product.
- Economic use of minerals.
- Substituting the use of rare and costly minerals with those which are abundant and cheaper.

The conservation of mineral resources does not mean preservation of minerals underground to be used by future generations but it implies efforts to utilize minerals in best possible way, depending upon the industrial needs and changing technological requirements, so that the life of the deposits is increased without sacrificing out own needs. From the utilization point of view, minerals are placed under two classes: expendable and non-expendable. Expendable minerals have practically no salvage value and one consumed are lost for ever, e.g., petroleum, gas, and most of the non-minerals. Non-expendable minerals and those which have good salvage value and can be used again through recycling, except those quantities that are lost due to corrosion and abrasion, e.g. metallic minerals.

A facility (house, hospital, port) or even in providing a service to society (medical care, public transport). Firewood, fuels (coal, petroleum and its products natural gas) solar energy, biogass, wind and hydropower, and atomic power and chief energy resources. Of these, firewood and fossil fuel are being used for supply of energy since time immemorial and are known as conventional energy sources. Wind and hydropower, solar energy, biogass and atomic energy are the new and nonconventional source of energy. Fossil begin limited in supply may be termed as exhaustible sources while other, like solar, hydel wind and atomic energy that would be available to man for infinite period are regarded as inexhaustible sources, firewood and other biofuels such as biogas derived from biological wastes, ecological implications since are already short of forests and whatever forests available should not be squeezed or thinned. However, use of other biofuel is known to be the best option in the light of two important facts: their steady or even increasing supply at low coast; their use in energy production reduces pollution of environment.

Because of rapid depletion and poor regeneration of the exhaustible sources of energy the society should concentrate on traping the inexhaustible and renewable sources under strict economic and ecological consideration.

Energy Sources

Fossil fuels, coal, petroleum, natural gas are the most extensively used sources of energy today. Like for many other natural resources, increase in population and per capita energy demand coupled with the industrialization at a faster pace, are the factors responsible for depletion of fossil fuel world over. According to a report the earth's original stocks of coal and petroleum were about 6,000 billion tons and 1,250 billion barrels respectively, of which by the year 1960,100 billion tons of coal was mined and 100 billion barrels petroleum extracted. The story of natural gas is no different which has acquired the status of irreplaceable commodity of domestic use in modern times. Petroleum and natural gas today fulfil 60 per cent of the world's total energy requirements. It is evident that if the exploitation and consumption of these resources continues at the present incredible rate, there supply may last only for a few more decades.

Non-conventional Energy Sources

The rapid depletion of conventional energy sources has prompted governments and people to concentrate on finding and tapping some non-conventional energy sources that may last for long. In fact, inexhaustible energy sources, like solar hydel tidal wind and atomic power, can only bring hope for the unsustained socio-economic development of humanity for years to come when exhaustible sources will become either inaccessible or too costly to afford.

Solar Energy

Research and application in the field of solar energy have opened new vistas in the direction of fulfilling world's future energy requirements. It has especially drawn attention for its practically free steady supply and pollution free use. This energy may be transformed into heat using reflectors and condensers, or into electric energy using solar photovoltaics. The resource can especially be tapped more effectively in the regions where there are long sunshine hours.

Solar heaters and cookers are becoming popular these

days in industry and house hold. Passive solar architectures provide comfortable housing in extreme cold and hot climates. This engineering has also been successfully applied in warehouses and cold storages. A multipurpose solar dryer-cum-warehouse is under construction at Ganau (Haryana, India) where chillies, potato-chips and other foodstuffs could be dried and stored. Solar energy has also been effectively used in desalination of water. College of Engineering Pune has designed a solar furnace that can generate heat upto 2,000°C which can be used in various metallurgical and other purposes.

The department of Nonconventional Energy Sources of Government of India has prepared a perspective plan that envisages generation of energy through nonconventional sources, chiefly solar, to the extent of 250 million tons of coal replacement per annum including 15,000 MW of electricity by the year 2001. India's first solar power station, soon to be operated near New Delhi, would be a great breakthrough in this direction. Rural electrification through solar photovoltaics is already in operation at some places in the country. Moreover photovoltaic irrigation pump sets have also been installed at some places.

Wind Power

The power of wind since olden days is being used in running mills, irrigation of fields, and out other farm activities, but its real potential is not so far being realized. According to inventories of Department of Nonconventional Energy Source of Government of India 2,000 MW electricity can be generated from the wind alone in the country. Wind power plants are set up in various parts of the country but they still account for the total capacity of 33 MW only. Obviously, this potent resource is to be tapped optimally.

Hydropower

In fact, use of gravitational flow of water in generation of electricity what commonly known as hydropower of hydel power, is quite common in various parts of the world. In India, first hydropower station, having a potential of 300 KW, was constructed at Darjeeling. Later on, many stations with far high potentiality were set up. The country's economically exploitable hydropower resources have been estimated at 41 million KW (or 41,000 MW) of which only 18 per cent of the potential was utilized by 1989. The Brahmputra basin has the highest hydropower potential and nearly 30 per cent of the country's total: next to it rank the Indus, Godavari, and Ganga basins respectively.

In world, a total of 4.910 x 10 KW electric power is generated of which hydropower from a fourth. In highly industrialized countries like USA, USSR, Canada, Japan, France, Sweden, and Norway hydropower is nearly fully developed whereas in the rest of the world it is yet to be developed fully.

Hydel power is considered to be the cheapest source of electricity with the cost of generation ranging from 2 to 3 paise per unit, compared to a minimum of 5 paise per unit of electricity generated by coal based thermal power.

Although the initial cost of hydel project is generally 25 per cent higher but owing to lower recurring costs the cost of generation of hydropower is the lowest. Apart from such economic considerations, development of such projects is beneficial for irrigation and other purposes too.

Tidal power of water in coastal areas of India is however, not so far being realized. According to an estimated tidal power potential of 9,000 MW has been identified, of which 7,000 to 8,000 MW is in the Gulf of Cambay, 800 to 1,000 MW in the Gulf of Kutch, and rest in Sunderbans.

Nuclear Power

No doubt the fossil fuels being exhaustible such sources of energy are not to last for long with the current trend of consumption. Atomic power appears to be the only hope for large scale energy requirements when fossil fuels are exhausted. The reserves of atomic fuels are said to be over 10 times grater than fossil fuel and the advantage of former is that their very small amounts would produce enormous amount of energy. A ton of Uranium, for instance, would provide as much energy as 3 million tons of coal or 12 million barrels of oil. Atomic energy has its application not only in generation of electricity but has successfully been used in marine vessels, spaceships, and even in chemical and food processing industry.

Important constraints in atomic energy generation are: (i) cost of construction and maintenance of plants and (ii) disposal of radioactive wastes. Cost of construction of an atomic power plant and its maintenance is very high as compared to any other electric power plant. Further, as a consequence of frequent failures, the running cost of such plants come to be very high. Moreover, after the working capacity of an atomic power plant is over (in about 25 years), these have to be destroyed so as to avoid radiation spillage. Surprisingly, the cost and time for destruction of these plants is almost equal to that for construction. Disposal of radioactive wastes is such a problem that still has no satisfactory solution for long term.

Bioenergy (Energy from biological matter); Organic wastes provide an important renewable source of energy. Biogas generated from the decomposition of organic wastes, like manure and domestic wastes, is becoming increasingly popular as a source of heat and light in many parts. It is considered to be advantageous in view of its relatively cheaper supply, and use of organic waters in its generation reduces the otherwise impending threat of pollution due to their release in environment. As such, it serves two purposes—fuel production and waste disposal. It has more of practical applicability in village where organic waste in the form of cattle dung is available in plenty. Biogas so generated is thus economic and convenient to use as compared to conventional practice of burning of dry dung-cakes. Further, the dung-cakes serve only as a source of heat for cooking and allied purposes while biogas has multifarious applications. The slurry as produced in a biogas plant can well be used as manure for agriculture fields.

Under the National Biogas Development Programme, 82 lac biogas plants were setup by the year 1985-86 in different parts of the country. A large-scale urban waste recycling plant at Okhla (New Delhi) generates about 0.6 million cubic feet gas per day having heat value of 700-800 BTU per cubic foot. The gas is being supplied to about 800 households. This project is gradually loosing ground. Despite best efforts this scheme can be popularised.

3

Environmental Demand Theory

First it is pertinent to note that the consumer preferences for goods (both for market goods and environmental goods) is the backbone of all economic phenomena. This is represented through demand functions, which shows a relationship between individual's desire for certian goods at a given level of income at a particular set of prices. Demand function is also known as 'demand curve' (when drawn as graph). Thus, it shows an inverse relationship between price of good and preference for good. The demand for good decreases/increases with the increase/decrease in price.

It must be remembered that by these informations one can easily understand the markets and the effect of changes in those markets. One can easily estimate the market's overall consumption of a particular good by an aggregate demand curve, the sum of individual demand curves. However, this can be matched with supply curve to analyse the equilibrium and the Hects of governmental in terventions through taxes and regulations in those markets, similarly, a demand curve can also be useful in summarizing preferences for environmental goods.

In the case of demand curves for environmental good, the basic problem is that there is no markets, so we have no observations on how much an environmental good is consumed at different prices. Yet, there is no doubt about the validity of demand theory (curve) for environmental goods, though it is just difficult to measure.

We shall now focus at demand theory for environmental goods. However, there is no significant difference in demand theory for conventional goods and services and environmental goods. Yet there are some typical extensions.

Speciality of an Environmental Good

It is well known that there are vast variety of environmental goods. Air pollution and water pollution, beautiful land and ocean vista, smoggy vista over a city etc., may be put under the category of commodity while 'air quality,' 'water quality' are viewed as environmental goods. Even more distant from the conventional notion of a good might be the existence of a species (which is important to many people) or the lives of particular members of a species (such as birds or fishes that might be killed in an oil spill).

The biggest problem to economists is to bring all aspects of environment for which consumer express their preferences comprehensively in the purview of paradigm of economic theory. The reason for doing this is that all environmental problems really involve a trade-off between using resources (money) for conventional goods and services and using those same resources for environmental protection.

In short, we are concerned about the quantity of money which a consumer is willing to spare (spent or give up) for particular levels of an environmental good. The protection from environmental pollution requires money. And it is pertinent to know the number of people who are willing to contribute to protect that environmental good.

However, it is difficult to estimate the true value, but it does not diminish the validity of the principle of demand for environmental goods and services. The existence of a market clearly shows the difference between ordinary goods and environmental goods. In the case of first, there is a market while in the second case there is no market. Hence, it is more difficult to generate a demand curve for environmental goods like clean air in an urban area than that to a market good, because of the non-existence of observations on different consumption levels and prices.

Yet clearly, individuals who value clean air would certainly be willing to pay for it. The more expensive clean air is to provide, the more people would be willing to tolerate some pollution (as they can not afford to spent for it); similarly, the cheaper clean air is, the more of it people would demand.

It is apt to mention that like public goods (e.g. schools, hospitals etc.), deriving demand curve for environmental good becomes difficult in the absence of market. But it is the supply side which clearly differentiates the environmental goods from ordinary public goods. Ordinary public goods are produced at cost. Thus, people do have a reference point of the cost of supply to take into account when determining quantity of goods to be purchased by them at particular prices.

However, this should not impact the value of consumption, it can make the process of valuation easier. On the contrary, environmental goods are often not connected from the supply side. In determining how useful he protection of a wilderness area might be, it is difficult to anchor that value, as the wilderness area is not produced. Air quality is in fact supplied, since there is a cost associated with cleaning up the air.

However, this is a much more dispersed cost, much different than that associated with constructing a public school or a park. This too makes the job of determining demand more difficult and complex.

Concept of Willingness to Pay

Now we shall try to apply the various concepts like demand curve, consumer surplus (developed in the presence of a market) for environmental goods in the absence of markets. The key concept corresponding to price and surplus is willingness to pay. We shall first attempt to show as how willingness to pay is analogous to price and then show how total willingness, to pay is analogous to consumer surplus.

1. Marginal Willingness to Pay (MWTP) and Prices

In fact, it should be worthwhile to note here that in this figure, the vertical axis shows MWTP (Marginal Willingness to pay) instead of price, the variable used in a conventional demand curve. Obviously, there can be no price in the absence of a market. But it is clear that these two terms—marginal willingness to pay and price, are equivalent. This can again be explained by taking an example from a market Suppose a consumer wants to know his marginal willingness to pay for one more unit of a commodity if its price is given as Rs. 10 per unit, in a limited time period (say one month). Now, consumer will try to decide the quantity to be consumed at this price. The consumer goes on increasing his consumption till he feels that the next unit of consumption's value is equal to the Rs. 10. price. The result of this experiment is for a consumer buying a good in a market, the value of one more unit of commodity to the consumer is exactly the price. In case, the consumer chooses to buy 20 units at a price of Rs. 10. per unit, in a month, the consumer's marginal willingness to pay for one more unit has to be Rs. 10.

It is apt to note that all demands curves for individuals show this fact. Each point on demand curve indicates for a particular quantity of the good, how the consumer values one more unit of the good—the marginal willingness to pay. In market, it is fundamental that for every consumer the price is the marginal willingness to pay. Here it makes no difference whether consumer is acquiring one more unit of good or giving up a unit. In case, the consumer is given up a unit that is possessed (e.g. selling an unit of commodity), the appropriate term is *marginal willingness* to accept compensation (MWTA). In most contexts, these two concepts are equivalent.

Remarkably, the case of pollution, we generally use the terms like *'damage from pollution'* or "the *benefit of having less pollution."* The marginal benefit of one less unit of pollution is the same as the marginal damage of one more unit of pollution. Remember that benefits of less pollution are the other side of the coin of damages from more pollution. When expressed in monetary terms, these benefits and damages are simply willingness to pay, making sure that the sign (positive or negative) is correct.

2. Willingness to Pay Versus Marginal Willingness to Pay

In fact, it will be necessary for a scholar to have a clear concept about the two terminologies oftenly used in the context of pollution—total damage from pollution or total benefits from reducing pollution. Besides this, one should have a clear distinction between total damage/benefits and marginal damage/benefits, or to use the earlier discussed terms, *total willingness to pay* and *marginal willingness to pay*. Let us explain these two terms by taking the case of Mumbai, a highly air polluted city. Now, if an individual citizen thinks to eliminate all air pollution from the city. This would be the total willingness to pay to eliminate air pollution. It is the same as the damage (in monetary units) to the individual from all of the air pollution in Mumbai City, similarly, one can also consider the willingness to pay to eliminate one unit of air pollution. This would be the marginal willingness to pay for reduction of air pollution. Remember 'price' can be used interchangeably with 'marginal willingness to pay.' Similarly, the area under the demand curve between two different quantities of the commodity shows the willingness to pay for the environmental commodity since no payment is made for the pollution (as there was for petrol), this is also consumer surplus (thorough note that it is negative).

3. Main Types

In fact, environmental goods can be grouped in several ways—

(a) According to the nature of the pollution air quality is one good, while water quality is another good.

(b) Classification based on the nature of injured party health effects of pollutions, damage to agriculture, and damage to buildings and materials.

(c) Classification based on how people perceive the damages. This classification is a bit more subtle and is related to achieving the utility from the environment by "using" the environment (e.g., linking through the woods) or through more esoteric means (e.g., thinking about "Anakonda" moving in deep lake in Arizona), by consumers.

1. Use Value

In common parlance, consumption of a good depends on the use value of a good. However, in the case of environmental good, this may include current use ("I am currently visiting a sea beach"), expected use ("I plan to visit the sea beach later this summer"), and possible use

("I might visit the sea beach within five years"). Although this might be clear, the point about possible use can be used to generate a positive value for a remote wilderness that few currently use, particularly if the very long term is taken into account.

Humans are affected in several ways by environmental goods. One is through direct impact. Direct impact on health of breathing polluted air may be both mortality as well as morbidity. Its non-health effect is bad odors, noise, or visual effects. Smokes from the power plant make the visibility dim which, though not measurable, causes irritation and annoyance. People would be willing to pay some money to get rid of it, if opportunity rise. This is just as real an economic value as health effects. Similarly, on the production side, pollution may enter directly into production functions, adversely affecting production processes. Environmental goods may impact humans less directly, primarily through materials damage.

As such, environmental goods do impact humans through damage to ecosystems, from which humans directly derive benefits clearly the pollution that degrades the performance of these ecosystems is undesirable. Ecosystems are also helpful and valuable for its recreational and aesthetic values.

In fact, parks, beaches, water falls, etc., if not damaged by pollution, have recreational as well as economic value. Not only this, ecosystems are also a source of economic benefit through mechanisms such as providing generatic material for new pharmaceuticals.

2. Nonuse Value

Non-use value is nothing but a gain in individual's utility without the individual actually using the good. Here "using" word is used in very broad sense. One may value ecosystems in remote area of the world not as he/she intend to visit the ecosystem or potentially achieving something from the ecosystem, but for other reasons, which may make him/her feel god (gives him/her utility).

We may value a *chaultry* (Dharamshala) near holy pilgrims of Haridwar, Kedarnath, not because we plan to make use of the chaultry, but because others may, and that makes us feel good (gives us utility).

Remarkably, existence value, altruistic value, and bequest value are the three basic types of non-use value.

As such, existence value is the value a consumer attaches to knowing something exists (e.g. the African Anakonda). This would, however, be in addition to any value associated with actual or potential 'use'. Altruist value derives not from one's own consumption but from the fact that he derives benefit when some one else gains utility. So if our neighbour derives benefit from our putting an electrical bulb on the light pole, we obtain utility from the fact that our neighbour is better off.

Bequest value is similar, though associated with the well-being of descendants. For example, if we value passing a sea beach on the next generation, that sea-beach has a bequest value to us, even if we never use it or intend to use it.

It must be remembered that all these exercise of placing the values in different categories is done with the objective of making the complexity easily comprehensible whereby environmental goods confer value on consumers. Similarly looking at the use value of an environmental asset may obscure much of the value. Empirically it is difficult to measure separately the components of value, for instance, how much value is altruistic vs. bequest.

The classification simply provides an intellectual frame

work to help ensure completeness when valuing environmental goods and services.

4. Measurement of Demand

Measuring the demand for environmental goods is not straightforward because of the absence of markets. However, this, can be measured either by revealed preference approach or by stated preference approach. In revealed preference, one observes a real choice in some market and wisely draws information on the trade-off between money and the environmental good.

It can be easily inferred after looking the price differences of houses, that people place the value to clean air. In stated preference approach, people are required to tell about the worth of environmental goods to them. This information is drawn from opinion polls and surveys. Because of the absence of real choices this approaches controversial.

Only real choices involve actual trades between money and environmental goods due to lack of realism in hypothetical choicing one can not get accurate informations.

It is apt to mention that there are two basic approaches—hedonics and household production, in revealed preference. In hedonic approach attempt is made to know the amount of changes in the price of conventional goods (e.g. a house) due to change in environmental good (e.g. the air quality). From this value is inferred. In household production approach it is assumed that consumers will combine private goods with the environmental goods to "produce" another good, which is the real source of utility.

For instance, to keep the indoor noise to tolerable limits (which matters), one can apply sound proofing in/out of his house to avoid noise pollution. The amount spent on sound proofing (private good) we can know the value of environmental god or bad. The outside noise must cause at least as much damage as the expenditures on sound proofing.

Contingent valuation is the main approach in stated preferences. It relies on direct revealation of demand from consumers. The name literally means "value contingent on there being a market"—if there were a market, how much would you pay for the environmental good? These values are obtained by directly questioning a sample of potential consumers of the environmental good.

Oftenly people use the term "constructed market" for contingent valuation. In a constructed market, a researcher will assume a situation in which there is no market and generate a market. Constructed markets can be hypothetical or real. For instance in a study of duck hunting, *Bishop* et al. (1983), constructed a market for buying and selling duck hunting permits (the permits were normally distributed through a lottery). In this manner they were able to generate a demand curve for duck hunting permits. Similarly, Shogren *et al.* (1994) study of the value of risk reduction is very important.

Further, official referendum is another type of constructed market. In this method. Some environmental good is to be provided using a tx on residents of a community. The proposal is put to the voters of a community. Although this is a very real choice situation, its usefulness is obviously limited to the environmental goods offered to communities through referenda.

5. Consumer Demand

It is pertinent to note that the study/analysis in this section presumes that reader is well-versed with the demand theory for conventional goods. This section is restricted to the demand theory related to environmental goods only.

1. Restricted Demand

Unlike conventional gods, the quantity of environmental goods, or public goods is not chosen by the consumers. But the demand and expenditure functions for environmental good 'q' will remain same with certain modification in conventional good model. Here, we shall use the quantity "q" of environmental good instead of the price of q. Thus, our ordinary demand function for the conventional market good z will be X_z (p_z, 1, y) and the compensated demand function will be h_z (p_z, q, v). We might for instance, observe the demand for boat rentals (z), and see that it depends on the price of boat rentals and water quality (q).

The expenditure function in this case is:

$$tE(p_z, q, v) = p_z h_z(p_z, q, v) \qquad \text{... (1)}$$

In case of there being more market goods, Eqn. (1) would simply have additional terms representing the other market goods.

Here, z and q are two goods,

p_z is price of z,

v is particular level of utility

y is income.

Notice that the demand functions and expenditure functions are very similar to before, except that the quantity of q appears rather than the price of 1. This type of demand and expenditure functions are called as *restricted demand and expenditure functions.*

Because of the relationship between q and E, the restricted expenditure function will make a lie to the conventional expenditure and demand functions. This can be explained through an example. Suppose an individual purchases few commodities including 10 packets of biscuits priced at Re. 1 each. The total cost of all the commodities is Rs. 40, (Rs. 10 for biscuits and Rs. 30 for other commodities).

Now, suppose one does not observe the price of biscuits and see the expenditure of Rs. 30. On other commodities, when you have 10 packets of biscuits in your bag. The question is, can we determine the worth of biscuits to that particular individual by observing his demand for other commodities?

This is similar to observing demand for market goods when consuming a non-market environmental good; on problem is finding the value of the environmental good. The answer is alternative. The value of one more packet of biscuit can be determined. Think of a situation in which you are given one more packet of biscuit and notice that you are not required to spent d more on other commodities to keep utility constant. We see from your compensated demand function for the other commodities how much income must be taken away to keep utility constant. This will be your marginal valuation of a packet of biscuit. It Rs. 1 has to be taken away to make up for the extra utility from the extra packet of biscuit, the value of that extra packet of biscuit is obviously Re. 1.

Now, we turn to the restricted expenditure function (Eqn. 1) to know the impact of a little increase of Δq in q. As q is desirable, utility will rise unless we educe the income accordingly. The ratio of the change in the expenditure function to the change in q is the value of *q at the margin.*

This is the marginal willingness to pay for q. It is denoted by p_q. If 1 were offered on the market at this price, and income were supplemented by $p_q q$, the amount chosen voluntarily would be exactly q.

Thus, we have a *connection between compensated demand and the restricted expenditure function.*

$$\Delta E\ (p_z q.u)/\Delta q = -p_q \qquad \text{... (2)}$$

This can be rearranged as

$$q = h_q\ (p_z, p_q, u) \qquad \text{... (3)}$$

which is compensated demand function for q.

Consider the compensated demand curve for our market god, $z{:}h_z(p_z,q,u)$. Assume that price of z happens to be p_Z^* and the amount of 1 is q_o. This demand curve is show in Fig (4.3), alongwith the quantity of z that will be consumed, z*. Now, change q by Δq to become $(q_o + \Delta_q)$. As q being the environmental good, is very much desirable. For keeping utility to remain constant it is essential to decrease the quantity of z when q is increased. The resulting compensated demand curve for $(q+_o + \Delta_q)$ is also shown in Figure 4.3), slightly below the original demand curve. The headed (dotted) area in this figure shows the compensating income equivalent to change in q.

This can also be called in q. The significance of above findings lies in is implication for finding out a demand curve for environmental good (even if we do not have market for it) from demand curve for ordinary good.

Measurement of Welfare Effects

In fact, one can advantageously use the compensating and equivalent variation (change) to assess the welfare effects of changes in the quality of environment. Let us start that an individual consumes q_o (level of environmental quality) to obtain U_0 (utility) when his income is Y. Now, if environmental quality changes to q_1, the individual will now be at utility level U_1.

What is the value of environmental changes? One method of valuing the action that changed quantities is to obtain the amount of money, corresponding to the action, that would have the same effect on utility.

The amount of money that would keep the individual at the original level of utility with the change is the *compensating surplus* and the amount of money that would move the individual to the new level of utility without the change is called the *equivalent surplus.* These two terms are analogous to compensating and equivalent variation in the case of a market good. Here we have used the term "surplus" instead of "variation," because consumer is not free to change the quantity of 1. For all other things, the concepts are identical.

The above to terms can be defined by using expenditure functions of conventional good. The compensating surplus of moving from q_o to q_o is denoted by CS (q_o, q_1) and $ES(q_oq_1)$ is the analogous equivalent surplus i.e.,

$$CS\ (q_o,q_1) = E(p_zq_o,U_o) - E(p_z,q_1,U_o) \quad \text{... (4)}$$

$$ES(q_o,q_1) = E(p_z,q_o,U_1)\text{-}E(p_z,q_1,U_1) \quad \text{... (5)}$$

Equation (4) is the compensating surplus. It is defined as the difference in income needed to achieve the old level of utility at the old quantity $[(p_z,q_o,U_o)]$ and the income needed to keep the same level of utility at the new quantity $(E(p_z, q_1,U_o)]$.

Similarly, equivalent surplus, is the change in income that would have the same ("equivalent") effect on the quantity change, without the quantity change actually occurring. In other words, we should compare the expenditures that yield utility U_1 at the original quantity with the expenditures necessary to yield utility U_o at the original quantity.

$$ES(1_o,q_{1)\ =\ E(p}z,q_o,U_1)\text{-}E(p_z,q_o,U_o) \quad \text{... (6)}$$

Which is actually the same as Equ. (5) because, $E(p_z, q_1, U_1) = E(p_z, q_0, U_0)$.

AB and CD are indifference curves showing utility levels U_0 and U_1 at quantities q_0 and q_1;

ES is equipment surplus;

CS is compensating surplus;

p_s is the price of environmental good;

$y = p_z Z$ is budget constraint

These definitions are subtle and are difficult to understand. Hence, some simpler examples are needed to explain these two concepts.

Suppose Venkatesh lives near the sea coast, from where he has a nice view. Now, if Alexander purchasing the land between Rama's house and sea coast wants to built a house, which will block the nice view of sea coast to Venkatesh . Now, there are two ways to view the money equivalent of the damage to Venkatesh from the house built by Alexander. *First,* Venkatesh pays maximum amount of money to Alexander not to build the house. Now Venkatesh would only pay that amount of money such that his income after the payment and with a clear view of the sea coast results in the same utility as his income without the payment and without the view. This is the equivalent surplus—a money measure that is equivalent to the loss of the view. Venkatesh actually will remain indifferent between paying this amount to prevent the loss of the view and not paying but loosing the view.

Second way of looking at the value would be if there is any rule/law in the area, which prohibits any construction which obstructs another's view without permission of the viewing party. Accordingly, Alexander will have to pay Venkatesh for this right. Alexander should pay that amount of money to Venkatesh so that Venkatesh's utility with the payment but without the view is the same as with no payment but no blocked view—in other words Venkatesh's original level of utility. This is the compensating surplus—Alexander has to compensate Venkatesh for the loss of utility from taking away his view.

However, compensating surplus and equivalent surplus are the same for small value relative goods. Sometimes income effect may cause difference between them.

REFERENCES

Bishop, R.C., Thomas A.H., and Mary J.K., "Contingent Valuation of Environmental Assets: Comparisons with Simulated market", *N.R.J.*, 23:619 - 633 (1983).

C.D. Kolstad, *Env. Eco.*, pp. 298-304.

Shogren, J.F., Senng, Y.S., Dermot, J.H., and James, B.K., "Resolving Differences in Willingness to Pay and Willingness to Accept., *A.E.R.*, 84 : 253-270 (1994).

4

Macroeconomic Policies and Environment

It is apt to mention here first that eternal inter-dependence of economic development (via economic policies) and environment is the theme of this chapter. One can not expect the eradication of environmental degradation without proper economic resources (capitalised and used) development. On the contrary it is also not feasible (possible to some extent) to achieve development with the depleted natural resource. Hence, economic policies and environment bear a kit and kin relationship.

ENVIRONMENTAL AND DEVELOPMENTAL COMPROMISES AND SUSTAINABLE DEVELOPMENT

In fact, the degradation of environment caused by the rapid industrial growth during the tast three decades ad various developmental compromises due to national and international pressures, have caused concern to the close relationship between environment and tradable economic activities, apart from massive resource depletion. According to D.H. Meadows, D.L. Meadows and R. Ramders, there are a number of non-renewable resources which will not last longer with present level of consumption. Similar findings are also obtained in many other studies.

Thus, "environmental protection" has now become the focal point. According to World Development Report (1992), environmental problems undermine the goals of development in two ways: "First, environmental quality-water that is safe and plentiful and air that is healthy—is itself part of the improvement in welfare that development attempts to bring. If the benefits from rising incomes are offset by the costs imposed on health and quality of life by pollution, this cannot be called development.

Second, environmental damage can undermine future productivity. Soils that are degraded, aquifers that are depleted, the ecosystems that are destroyed in the name of raising incomes today can jeopardize the prospects for earning income tomorrow." This clearly indicates that environmental conservation should invariably form a party of any comprehensive programme of industrial development. In this context, the concept of *Sustainable Development* is being more emphasised.

In fact, the term—Sustainable Development—was for the first time came into coinage in the World Conservation Strategy in 1980 by the International Union for the Conservation of Nature and Natural Resources. This was defined in Brundtland Report *Our Common Future.* In 1987 in these words: "Sustainable development seeks to meet the needs and aspirations of the present without compromising the ability of future generations to meet their own needs."

It is significant to note that achievement of sustainable development is only possible if the environment is conserved and improved. Therefore, a development path is sustainable "if and only if the stock of overall capital assets remains constant or rises over time. More strictly, "the requirement is for non-negative change in the stock of natural resources and environmental quality. In basis terms, the environment should not be degraded further but improvements would be welcome." The basic fact behind this is that the resource base of a country and the quality of its air, water and land represents a common heritage for all generations. The destruction of this endowment for short term business gains compromising the future generation's gains, is thus undesirable.

Therefore, it is imperative for the government to incorporate some form of *environmental accounting* into is policy decisions. This requires that "the preservation or loss of valuable environmental resources should be factored into estimates of economic growth and human well-beings. Alternatively, policy makers may set a goal of no net loss of environmental assets.

In other words, if an environmental resource is damaged or depleted in one area, a resource of equal or greater value should be generated elsewhere."

INTEGRATED ENVIRONMENTAL AND ECONOMIC ACCOUNTING

It is pertinent to note that conventional national income accounting system do not fully in corporate the depletion of natural resources and the degradation of the environment. Thus, this does not send correct/right signals to the policy makers. To overcome this difficulty, the statistical Division of the United Nations has been working to supplement the system of National Accounts with a *Satellite System of Integrated Economic and Environmental Accounting.*

These experimental accounts involves some innvations. One of the most concern is expenditure for environmental protection. Since each spending compensates for the negative impact of economic growth, it is considered to be a cost, to be substracted from national income. These satellite accounts incorporate both-standard balance sheets and income accounts in improved/complete form. For this, first step for a country is to draw up a comprehensive balance sheet of natural resources measured in physical quantities.

For some of these resources it is also possible to impute a monetary value which can be added to physical capital to from an expanded capital account. Give zero value to the non-scarce resources. In this new accounts system, depletion of capital will not only include depreciation of physical capital, but also depletion of natural resources, alongwith the deterioration of environmental quality. When drawing up national income accounts, these environmental losses can then be substracted to produce a new measure of growth—environmentally adjusted/corrected domestic product.

It is remarkable that several countries have tested this new system of accounts. For Mexico in 1986-90, it was found that environmental adjusted domestic product was 13 per cent less than the conventionally measured net domestic product. The new accounting measures also showed that net investment—Which conventional measures showed as positive, at 46 billion pesos—was negative 700 million pesos. Net savings, also assumed to be positive, was actually close to zero. Papua New Guinea Case study in the some period showed the same results. There, consumption, exceeded out put, so that net savings were negative.

Macro-economic Policies and Environment

As is obvious, economic development of a country depends mainly on the way how that country utilises/ explores her national resources, viz. natural and human etc. In this process, rapid industrialisation plays important role. This mad race of industrialisation and technological development intesifies the environmental problems in three ways.

First, as emissions from existing activities increase, they pass the point at which they can be rapidly assimilated by the environment.

Second, as the industrial towns expand, more people are exposed to pollution.

Third, within the industry the structure shifts away from the activities that are moderately polluting, such as textiles, wood products and food processing, and toward others with much greater potential for causing environmental harm, such as metals, chemicals, and paper.

The organic wastes in water effluents and toxic wastes emitted by large industries are major source of pollution. Small and medium-scale industries, which provide employment and production do cause the pollution on the same line as in large industries. Apart from this, human activities and domestic wastes do cause pollution. On the other hand, no economic activities in a country can be endeavoured without proper economic policy. Economic policies—both macro and micro, play significant role in determining the economic environment in a country.

Besides this, internal environment, which includes value system, goal and objectives, management structure, relationship among the various constituents, physical assets, technological capabilities and human, financial and marketing resources, and *external environment,* which includes institutions, organisations and forces operating outside the industries, do play significant role in formulation and conducting of economic/non-economic activities in the country.

All these individually as well as collectively influence

the economic environment. From the point of view of the industrial operations micro-economic policies (i.e. micro environment has great relevance. The policies related to inputs supply, workers, customers, public, competitors, marketing intermediaries, etc. constitute the micro environment.

In fact, the macro-environment, which includes all the activities/factors—economic and non-economic, exercise their influence on business/industrial activities. Basically, economic environment—both national and global—is of strategic importance. In the economic environment of the country country's economic system, macro-economic senario, economy's trade cycle phase, organisation of financial system and economic policy of the government are the most important elements.

Remarkably parameters of industrial/economic activity are determined by the economic system of the country. Macroeconomic Senario (resultant of macro-economic policies) refers to price situation, saving and investment levels, fiscal, monetary and balance of payments situation and overall growth activities.

These factors broadly determine the business/industrial activities. National and global economic environment do effect environmental depletion. Apart from this, non-economic environment which involves political system ideology of the government, legar framework, social system, cultural values, demographic factors, level of technological development, natural and physical situations etc. of a country. These factors not only determine opportunities for economic activities, but also, at times, have serious constraining effects.

It should be once again borne in the mind that environmental degradation and its conservation are the implications of various economic and not economic activities. These activities are resultant of various policies operating (formulated by the government) in the country. We will now discuss few important macro-economic policies which have direct bearing on environment macro-economic Policies:

> Economic policies of a government play significant role in the determination/creation of economic environment in a country. These policies can be broadly classified under four areas: (1) Industrial Policy, (2) Trade Policy (3) Monetary Policy, and (4) Fiscal Policy.

Industrial Policy and Environment

Notably, among various economic activities, industrial activities, determined/guided by industrial policy of the nation, are more directly related to the environment.

According to the Indian Industrial Policy (since 1956) both public and private sectors can run industries. There were 17 industries under state responsibilities. However, the public and private sectors were not totally independent of one another. In 1973, considerable concessions were given to private sectors units and foreign multinationals. The actual liberalisation process began in 1980. In this period, the limit of exemption from licensing was continuously raised. In order to encourage production, government delicesed 28 broad categories of industries, and 82 bulk drugs and their formulations, and gave various concessions to companies falling under MRTP Act and FERA.

Government also allowed capacity re-endorsement for improvement in utilisation capacity in industries. Besides, introducing the scheme of broad banding of industries in 1984, Government also announced various concessions to promote the expansion of exports.

Except for certain industries related to strategic and

social concerns, government abolished all industrial licensing to de-regulate the industrial economy in its New Industrial Policy of 1991. Limiting the number of public sector industries to 3, government expressed its concern in reduction of public sector role.

The MRTP has been replaced by new competition law. The new industrial policy has also liberalised import of foreign capital and technology, besides providing automatic approval of foreign to investment for high investment priority industries. It also provided guide-lines for the expeditious approval of foreign direct investment in others industries. After globalisation the entire scenario.

Trade Policy

Trade policy, which can be outward-oriented and inward oriented, is an important factor in formation of economic environment. The outward trade policy is more liberalised in nature because it neither discriminates between the production for domestic market and exports, nor between purchases of domestic goods and foreign goods. This compells the firms to efficient and internationally competitive. On the contrary inward oriented trade policy is biased in favour of domestic market. This approach is also known as the import substitution strategy. It encourages protection, nd survive over a long period without being internationally competitive but also make huge profits.

Due to the inward-oriented trade policy of India during 1951-91, its share was less than half a percent in world trade. As a result of this policy, India neither prosper industrially nor was independent on the external world. Trade grew at a meagre rate, The introduction of new exim-policy (import and export policy) in 1992, created international competitiveness in Indian business, as it reduced export pessimism. The failure on this front, may definitely cause a severe setback to it.

Fiscal Policy

It is the fiscal policy of a country, which shapes the taxation and public expenditure for controlling the fluctuations in trade cycle apart from contributing to rapid economic growth with high employment and price stability. A mis-managed fiscal policy may lead to to fiscal imbalances which at times become unsustainable. Last two decades of India faces this problem as its fiscal situation reached to precarious level. Due to ever increasing non-developmental expenditures through out eightees, the central Government's fiscal deficit reached to a level 6.6 percent of G.D.P. in 1990-91. Fiscal deficit at this level is unsustainable. However, over the last twenty years there has been good improvement in country's fiscal situation. Since fiscal deficit has to be financed by public borrowings which has a tendency to raise interest rates, credit is likely to be cheap in recent years.

Owing to this high cost of finance Indian trade/industries because disadvantageous in internation markets vis-a-vis other countries having relatively low interest rates. High rates of interests also attract foreign portfolio investment which, in turn, gives us overvalued exchange rate. An overvalued exchange rate undermines the competitiveness of our export in today's highly competitive international markets. Hence, it is necessary to make fiscal corrections for providing a stable background for the economy and offsetting major disturbances in economic system arising from different sources/avenues.

Monetary Policy

According to C. Rangarajan, "Monetary Policy is an arm of macro-economic policy and, as such, its role and importance are determined in any economy by the overall policy framework and the various instruments available for implementing policy." It is of great relevance to trades and industries because of its influence on cost and credit and money availability.

Its role in stabilisation of domestic economy fulfills the objective of improving country's exports in world trade, the need to service external debt and increase openness of the national economy in recent years. Price stability, however, in this context does not imply absence of any increase in prices. Likewise, the absolute price stability or zero inflation is not a goid thing. The costs of zero inflation are large. On the contrary, an inflation rate of 3-4 percent creates a good environment for business. The inflation rate in last ten years has been as high as 5.5 per cent. No credit squeeze policy can be adopted to contain inflation in the present recessionary climate as it can seriously hamper economic growth.

However, for improvement in trade environment in the country, inflation control is desirably advantageous. This purpose can be obtained by the government by adopting a prudent fiscal policy.

Non-Economic Macro-Policies

Though trade/industry is an economic activity, it is also affected by non-economic macro policies like (1) Political and Legal, (ii) Socio-cultural, (iii) Demographic, (iv) Technological and, (v) Natural.

It must be remembered that, political system and legal and law and order situations, on the one hand creates the peaceful, fluctuationless environment in the country, on the other hand provide protection for establishment of trade and industry in the country. It also create environment for foreign investment. Likewise, socio-cultural policies do promote tourism in the country which becomes a great source foreign exchange. Demographic policy related to size and growth rate of population is a great factor for creating the demand of goods and services and thus factors. This creates a viable environment for trade and industry.

No doubt, technological advancement and natural environment do cause establishment and promotion of trade and industry in the country.

Summing Up

From above discussion it can be surmised that that no business/trade or industry can either be established or flourish in the absence of suitable and congenial economic and non-economic environment created by national as well as international policies. But, once they are established, they trial to care for ecological effects of heir activities. Guided entirely by its profit maximization goal the industry causes tremendous damage to exhaustible natural resources as such minerals and forests. It also contaminates water and pollutes air. These externalities imposed by the industry on the society were mere overlooked both by the government and the people until such time the environmentalists and well-being by causing environmental damage. The trade/business has so far got away in most countries with its callous indifference towards environmental damage which its activities caused.

This may not be possible due to greater environmental awareness and state's effective control in future. In the case of happening of this, trade activities will have to be internalised. This implies that the social cost which industries/businesses presently impose on other will assume the form of private cost and make dent into its profits.

As such, it can be surmised that the existence of cause-effect relationship of vis-a-vis nature between deptetion of environment and control and macro-economic and non-economic policies causes concerns to the nation and the world. This has to be broken in the welfare of human community both at national and international levels.

REFERENCES

C. Rangarajan, *Indian Economy-Essays in Money and Finance* (N.D. UBS Publishers, Distributors Ltd., 1988), p. 59.

David W. Pearce and J. Warford, *World Without End: Economics, Environment and Sustainable Development: A Summary* (Washington, D.C., World Bank, 1993), p. 3.

David Pearce, Edward Barbier and Anil Markandya, "Sustainable Development: Ecology and Economic Progress,' (ed.) *Leading Issues in Economic Development* (New York : O.U.P., Seventh Ed., 2000), p. 555.

Meadows, D.H., Meddows, D.L. and Randers, R., *'The Limits to Growth,* 1972.

Michael P. Todaro, *Economic Development* (Reading Masachusetts. Addision-Wesley Longman, Inc., 2000), 411.

United Nations Development Programme, Human Development Report, 196 (N. Delhi: O.U.P., 1996), pp. 63-5.

World Bank, *World Development Report,* 1992 (N.Y. O.U.P. 1992), p. 1.

5

Ronald Coase's Theorem of Property Rights

"It is literally true that no man has ever used more than a small fragment of his brain power. ... Almost from birth we are continuously blocked by conflicts among in-ternal factions. Each man grows up to resemble a pair of moose with horns locked in battle. He dies of a strug-gle which he wages with himself."

—*Dr. Lawrence S. Kubie*

World Development Report (1992) points out that market failures occurs as markets frequently do not accurately reflect the social value of environment (and hence costs of environmental degradation).

Main Causes

- No market exists because it is difficult to demarcate or enforce the rights to own or use the environment—as with air quality. Thus, prices do not reflect the adverse effects of pollutants and the results is too much air pollution.
- Due to partial marketing of resources, non-marketed benefits are ignored whereas other uses of resources re overexploited.
- Open access to resources allow them to be exploited by all, without giving cognition to its environmental effect.
- Individuals as well as society lacks information about environmental impacts or about low cost ways to avoid damage.

As such, our main problem is to find out the ways to correct the market failure. Among various methods we will confined ourselves to correcting imperfect property rights—defining and establishing, in this chapter.

It is pertinent to note that according to some economists, the problem of market failure (externalities) arises due to defective property rights. The allocation of goods and bads efficiently by market depends on the properly defined property rights. According to Browning and Jacquelence, "the government may not need to use taxes, subsidies, or regulation at all; it need only define and enforce properly rights, and the resulting market exchanges would produce an efficient resource allocation. Should every body has the right to clean air, and in case of occurrence of pollution has the entitlement to elimination of the pollution or compensation for pollution damage. Or should polluters have the right to pollute?

It must be remembered that the answer to these questions are no as simple as it first appears. According to conventional view the blame should fall on the source of the problem i.e., on polluter. However, one would also blame the victim, (leading all preconceptions of right or wrong) as he is next to polluter. Without the victim, the pollution would not be a problem morally, the factory should be held responsible the cleaning up the pollution. It is possible to draw same conclusion by suing economic efficiency arguments.

Ronald Coase, the Nobel laureate in economics in 1960, raise the subtle issue of who should have rights, the polluter or the victim, in an important paper for which he achieved the prestigious prize. One of Coase, conclusions is that under some conditions, there is no difference to efficiency whether polluter has a right to pollute or the victim has a right to clean air (although it will make a great deal of difference to each of these two parties). As the right to pollute is a property right has value, and if trade is allowed in those rights, efficiency should prevail, no matter how they were initially allocated. In case, right is more worthy (valuable) for victim than polluter, the victim will end up with the right, no matter how it was initially, distributed. However, initial distribution of rights does matter to questions of equity. Rights can be valuable. Bestowing (giving) right is like giving them money and resources.

It is pertinent to note that Coase's arguments regarding property rights are often dubbed in Coase Theorem, falsely suggesting precision. Coase's Theorem has two parts. One where no restrictions on buying and selling pollution rights are applicable. Here, initial distribution of rights has no significance. Two, where trading of property rights are restricted. Not surprisingly, in this case the initial distribution of right is significant.

Generated Explanation of the Theorem

In fact, in the foregoing paragraphs we show that in easy bargaining between two parties case, pollution problem was solved without any leagal assignment of rights to a clean air/environment, which end up at the same spot in both cases. But easy bargaining assumptions between tow parties are not always possible. Also, there are some bargaining costs. However, there are some transaction costs, besides psychic costs (there are psychic costs associated with striking bargains with neighbouring diverse). The costs are just as real as monetary, costs and are supposed as impediment as transaction cost.

1. Assumptions of Coase Theorem

For explaining his property right Theorem Coase assumes a world in which some producers or consumers are subject to externalities generated by other producers or consumers.

The other assumptions are:

1. Every one has perfect information;
2. Producers as well as consumers are price takers;
3. There is a costless (free of cost) system for enforcing agreements,
4. Consumers maximise utility whereas producers maximizes profits;
5. There are no income or wealth effects;
6. And, there are no transaction costs.

In this case, the initial assignment of property rights regarding the externalities does not matter for efficiency. However, in the absence of any of these conditions or does not hold, the initial assignment of rights does matter or is significant.

2. Statement of Theorem

According to this Theorem, if there are no barriers to reaching agreement (such as breverage paying the cement factory not to pollute), we get efficiency, regardless of how property rights are initially distributed. In reality, Coase Theorem goes beyond externalities broadly to all market failures. In a monopoly where no barriers to agreement exists, consumers can simply pay monopolists to produce at the efficient level, sharing the gains in efficiency. The zero transaction costs assumption in the Coase Theorem is most significant condition. In all most all real world situations, practical application of Coase Theorem is hindered/limited due to the presence of significant transactions costs. In fact, Coase himself has stated that the case of zero transaction costs is of limited interest:

"We do not do well to devote ourselves to a detailed study of the world of zero transactions costs, like augurs dividing the future by the minute inspection of the entrails of a goose."

Coase via his Theorem tries to draw our attention away from efficiency arguments for providing explanation for the reasons of allocation of property rights in a particular way.

Robert D. Cooter (1987) points out that even in the absence of transaction costs, bargains are hindered (in the same way as in the presence of transaction costs) by some impediments. He further points out that in a bilateral negotiation with gains from consumating and agreement, the bargain may breakdown because of clear-cut division decision of the gains. Another instance is in the case of public bads, where no transaction costs appears, and where many affected parties must bargain with the polluter (for more detail explanation see next section).

3. Wealth Effect

Wealth effects occupies important place in Coase Theorem. It is the possession of rights which makes a person rich or poor. If one is endowed with a right having value, he is richer. If he is not endowed with that right, he is poorer. It is well known fact that demand for goods depends on our income consequently, the existence of wealth effects would generate differences in final bargain, depending on how rights were initially allocated. This is the reason for assumption(s) in our statement of Coase Theorem.

One should keep in mind that Coase has never said that properly right is not important. For Coase, the way of distribution of property rights dos not matter. If the right to clean air have been endowed to the citizens, it is well defined right. Although, polluters possession of right to use the ir for smoke, is well-defied right, even then people may think it to be unfair. Thus, Coase simply believes that in case trading in these rights is easy and costless, it does not matter how they are initially distributed, they will subsequently be treated so that they end up in the right hands.

4. Existence of Transaction Costs

According to Coase, where the rights are initially vested presence of transaction costs do matter. With transaction costs, the status quo tends to prevail. This means that in case when rights are initially established by the legal system it is important to vest rights in those parties that have the greatest need for those rights. One should not believe our trade to redistribute rights to pollute. Of course another conclusion may be that attention should be paid to reducing the transaction costs associated with trading rights to pollute.

Coase Theorem

It will be pertinent as well as advantageous to demonstrate Coase's result via example before stating his result more generally.

The Polluter and the Victim: Who Should have the Rights?

In the case of cement factory and breverage, let us try to analyse the impact if the right to pollute lies with cement factory or if breverage has the right to clean air. And to have a standard (point of reference) for comparison, attempt will also be made determine the correct amount of pollution as well as output of cement and breverage.

In our example, in the process of production of cement pollution is also emitted. Now the cost of cement output (C) and the pollution emission is $C_c(C)$, and that of breverage,

B, will be C_B (B, C). In this case C (Cement output) depresses the breverage output, holding inputs fixed. The prises of cement (P_C and breverage (P_B is determined by a larger market and thus can be assumed as fixed throughout.

(A) Determination of Efficient

First step in this process is setting up of the standard output for "internalizing" the externality. This can be done by the merging of the two firms. There will be no externality in case of single firm produces both cement and breverage. In this way, the profit maximising choices for this merged firm will be efficient as well as socially desirable. The profit of this merged firm will be:

$$\pi_m \text{ (C,B)}, = p_c C + p_B B - C_c(C) - C_B \text{ (B,C)} \qquad \dots (1)$$

Now, the optimality conditions for the profit maximising output quantities devoted by C* and B*, will be:

$$\frac{\Delta\pi_m}{\Delta C} = p_c - \frac{\Delta C_c(C + \Delta C)}{\Delta B} - \frac{\Delta C_B\,(B_1C + \Delta S}{\Delta S} \qquad \dots (2)$$

$$= \; p_c - mC_c(C) - mD_B\,(B,C) - O$$

$$= \frac{\Delta\pi_m}{\Delta C} = p_B - \frac{\Delta C_B(B + \Delta B, C)}{\Delta B} = p_B - MC_B\,(B,C) = 0 \dots (3)$$

Note here that in Eqn: 1 the cement factory portion of this firm contains two marginal costs i.e., one, for cement mC_c and two, for breverage, mD_B. It is expected here that both mC_c and mD_B are positive. This equation also shows that the price of cement should be equal to the marginal cost to both the breverage and cement, i.e. $mC_c + mD_B$.

Similarly, the standard condition for breverage will be at that point where price of breverage and marginal cost of breverage are equal (ref. Equ. 3).

However, the marginal conditions are not always significant. Equations (2, 3) does not show the desirability of shutting-down the cement factory or the breverage, except that there may be no solution to these equations for which B* > O and C* > O (i.e. both the are positive). Although, marginal conditions do not include the fixed costs, even then they may determine whether revenue of a firm is sufficient to cover costs. In case it is not fulfilled, there is no alternative to firm but to stop production.

In case of closure of breverage, there is no damage from pollution, so cement production will be chosen, so that price and marginal costs are equal, i.e.,

$$p_c - mC_c\,(C) \qquad \dots (4)$$

Denote this amount of cement as Co and this will give the profit π_m (Co, O).

Marginal Conditions

In the foregoing paragraphs, we determined the efficient amount of an externality. Now, we shall discuss the case of the two firms operating separately, that is, we will consider the two propertys rights regimes, viz., one in which cement factory possess the right to pollute, two, in which breverage enjoys the right to clean air. Besides this, the determination of output (production) level in these regimes will also be our main concern.

Breverage has Rights to Clean Air

In fact, in this case breverage has a right to a pollution free environment, which implies that cement factory must compensate breverage for any damage it does.

Now, breverage's profit will be maximum at the equality of price with its marginal cost of production, (whatever cement factory's production is), i.e.

$$\frac{\Delta\pi_B}{\Delta_B} = p_B - \frac{\Delta C_B(B+\Delta B,C)}{\Delta B} = p_B - MC_B\ (B,C) = 0 \quad \text{.... (5)}$$

$$\text{or,} \quad p_B = mC_B\ (B,\ C) \quad \text{... (6)}$$

In principle Equ. 6 can be solved for B, defining B(C), the amount of breverage being produced when cement factory produces the amount C.

Now, the damage of breverage would be the difference in profits for breverage when cement is not being produced (and no pollution) and the cement's product is C. Thus, the profits for the cement factory will be.

$$\pi_c(C) = p_c.C - C_c(C)\{\pi_B[B(O),O] - \pi_B\ [B(C),C]\} = 0 \text{ ....(7)}$$

Here, π_B (B,C) denotes the profit of the breverage when its production is B, while cement's production is C. Also B(C) is the breverage production when cement production is C. The term in braces in Equ. (7) is the damage to breverage when cement production is C. This damage has to be paid to the breverage, consequently, it decreases the profit of cement factory.

As such, the marginal profit for cement factory will be obtained by the equation.

$$\frac{\Delta\pi_C\ (C)}{\Delta C} = p_C - MC_c(C) + \frac{\Delta\{p_B B - [B(C),C]}{\Delta C} = 0 \quad \text{... (8)}$$

$$\text{Here,} \quad \frac{\Delta\pi_B[B(C),C]}{\Delta C} = \frac{\Delta\{p_B B - C_C[B(C),C]}{\Delta C} \quad \text{... (9)}$$

$$= p_B\frac{\Delta B}{\Delta C} - \frac{VC_B[B(C)+\Delta B,C]}{\Delta C}\frac{VB}{VC} - \frac{\Delta C_B[B(C),C+DC]}{\Delta C} \text{... (10)}$$

$$= [p_B - MC_B\ (B,C)]\Delta B/\Delta C\ MD_B\ [B(C),C] \quad \text{... (11)}$$

$= mD_B = mC_B\ [B(C),C]$ ... (12)

The first term in brackets in Equ. (7) shows that breverage profit at C - O, is a constant, so it does not change with the change in C. Hence, it does not enter in Eqn (8).

Secondly, the term in brackets in Eqn (11) is exactly zero. There is no role of revenue changes in determination of marginal damage to the breverage of extra cement.

The production amount of cement can be obtained by combining Eqn (8) with eqn. (12).

i.e., $p_c = mC_c(C) + mD_B\ [B(C), C]$ ... (13)

Here, the amount of breverage and cement are obtained by the eqn. (5) and eqn (13).

As such, in case cement factory creates *damage through pollution, it will pay those damages and the amount of cement and breverage will be efficient.*

Cement Factory has Right to Pollute

Let us now consider the case when breverage has no rights to clean air, then basic question that how much cement be produced, remains to be answered. This can be obtained, as usual, on the equality of price of cement and $mC_c(C)$. Let that quality of output of cement be Co. The breverage would be willing to pay nearly all that increased income $\{\pi_B\ [B(C),C] - \pi_B\ [B(C_o), C_o]\}$ to cement factory to reduce cement out put. This will decrease the costs of cement factory so that its total profits from producing C are:

$\pi_c(C) = p_cC - C_c(C) + \{\pi_B\ [B(C), C] - [B(C_o),C_o]\}$ ... (14)

This can be written as:

$$\pi_c(C) = p_c C - C_c(C) = \{\pi_B[B(O] - \pi_B\ (p(C),C]\}$$

$$+ \{\pi_B\ [B(O),\ O[= \pi_B\ [B(C_o)\ C_o]\} \qquad ...\ (15)$$

Here, the term s in the last set of brackets is equal a constant—the difference in breverage profit with no cement and breverage profits with the maximum amount of cement.

It is clear here that marginal conditions for choosing C and B are identical under either property rights regime. Furthermore, those conditions are the same as for a merged firm, with the externality eliminated. This is the fundamental conclusion of Coase, i.e., the initial assignment of rights vis-a-vis pollution does not matter for efficiency.

It is important to note here that distribution of resources definitely depends on the assignment of property rights, Although the marginal conditions for the cement factory. Here the same for the two different property rights regimes, the total costs and thus profits of the cement factory were quite different. Compare Equ. (9.7) and Equ (9.15). In case of cement factory having rights of property, its costs are significantly lower, by the amount the breverage paid to reduce pollution, possibly as much as {***$_B$[B(O),)]—***]B] [B(C]o]), C]o]]}. This is clearly the value of the property right to clean air and, in the "no rights" case, it is being purchased by the breverage from the cement factory. After the purchase, the two property rights regimes be comes identical.

As the total costs differ under the two property rights regimes, one can have various other outcomes from the different assignment of rights. *The first outcome* may be that the two firms might merge, in which case the externality would be eliminated, since the costs and benefits of pollution control would be within the same firm. The purchasing of one firm by the other firm is equivalent to the merger case.

Hence, cement factory will purchase the breverage from its power instead of paying a lump-sum to breverage for pollution damage.

BARGAINING IN CASE OF PUBLIC BADS

The fundamental problem in the case of public bads is to reach on a genuine agreement when there are number of people who have the right to pollute and one and only one polluting that. In this case polluting plant will have to compensate people for damage, in lump-sum amount, else there will be problem.

On the contrary, in se when rights to pollute is vested in the plant, the people living in the vicinity of plant (being harmed) will have to get together to pay the plant not to pollute. Here, the problems of reaching agreement among the people surrounding the plant are significant. As we shall see, no matter whom the property right is vested with, the basic problem is free-riding and truthful revelation of demand.

Coase's Bargaining Solution and Collective Action (Bargaining Within Groups

In previous section we saw that the Coase Theorem was most applicable in the case of bargaining of two firms or people. There was no problem of free-riding and negotiating costs. But, however, this does not hold in the case when bargaining is between more than two firms or people. There may be no bargain that is agreeable to all three or more people simultaneously, even when transaction costs are not present. In such case an additional problems arises for the Coase Theorem. This can be explained with an example. Before illustrating the example, it will be advantageous to explain the two economic concepts—The core, and the coalition, which will be used here in discussion.

The core: The "core" is the one of the fundamental concepts of exchange involving multiple agents. The concept of contract curve was developed by Edgeworth. It is a curve, which is achieved by joining the various tangency point of indifference curves of two parties/firms which enter the trade or exchange. (see any standard microeconomics book). The idea here was that both the agents/firms were operating under the same marginal rates of substitutions between the two goods. The Core in those exchange examples was the portion of the contract curve that yielded utility for both parties higher than their initial situation. For two people, this is the core of the exchange example—the set of allocation to which n body will object (as both are at better of position. However, individual will object if they can do better on their own).

The Coalitions

In the case of three or more people (entering into transaction), a little generalised of the same concept may be applied. The Core is still a piece of the contract curve. But here we say that for an allocation to be in the core no body individually will object to it (compared to their initial situation) and, furthermore, no grouping of agents (smaller than the while or the whole itself) will object to the allocation. These groupings are called "coalition." A coalition can be one person, all people involved, or anything in between. The appeal of coreis that it is an allocation with which every one is happy. No under-the-table (or above board) Collusion between as few of the agents, changes that—they cannot do any better.

POLICY IMPLICATIONS

Obviously, there are several clear policy implications of the Coase Theorem, few of them worth mentioning are:

1. The transaction costs play significant role in the

efficient distribution of rights to a clean air (environment). This implies that in designing a set of property rights for environment, it is important both to distribute them approximately and/or work to reduce the costs associated with trading those rights.

2. As markets for rights to pollute become increasingly common, it is important to pay attention to this device.
3. The victims of pollution should not be reluctant (disgusted) to pay polluters to reduce pollutions. However, who pays is (to a certain extent) a secondary issue. This is a conclusion of Coase Theorem that has yet to find wide acceptance in environmental policy.
4. Efficiency is also possible even if the victims paid to attain it.

As noted by Browning and Browning, many issues of great importance, such as defence, police protection, air and water pollution etc. are 'large group externalities' or public goods, and private markets will not function effectively in these areas government intervention. In such case Coase Theorem fails.

REFERENCES

Baumol and Oates (1988) cite a swedish example of a refinery damaging an automanufacturing plant. Negotiation between these parties took place to eliminate the Pareto-relevant externality.

Browning. E.E. and Jacquelene M. Browning, "Microeconomic Theory and Applications" (S.P. and Co., 3rd Ed. 189), p. 594.

Coase, R.H., "The Coase Theorem and the Empty Core: A Comment," *J. Law Economics,* 24: 183-187 (1981).

Cooter, R.D. "Coase Theorem" in J. Eatwell, M. Milgate, and P.

Newman (eds.). *The New Palgrave, A Dictionary of Economics* (Macmillan London, 1987).

Schulze, W. and Ralph C. d'Arge, "The Coase Proposition, Information Constraints and Long Run Equilibrium," Am.Eco. Rev., 64:763-772 (1974).

W.D. Report (1992) World Bank, pp. 64-65.

6

Effects of Environmental Regulations on Economy

> "If you lean back and close your eyes you can see things that happened years ago. But if you want any-thing to happen now, you'd better keep them open."
>
> —*Agnes Guilfoyle*

It is pertinent to note that the issue concerns properly accounting for environmental protection in our aggregate measure of economic performance, such as gross national product (GNP and productivity. A common feeling about this is that environmental regulations retard growth and "hurt" the economy. But standard measures of growth and economic health do not consider (omit) the benefits of a clean environment.

Further, one more issue concerns the impacts of environmental regulations on pre-existing inefficiencies in the economy, primarily due to taxes. This is a very delicate issue. Almost, everywhere in world, taxation is the greatest source of the economy particularly labour taxation).

Such taxes introduce distortions in the economy. And, now there are suggestions that pollution taxes be substituted for distortionary taxes, and that, as a result everyone will be better-of, even before the benefits of reduced pollution are taken into account. This is the so-called "double dividend" of environmental taxation. This is an optimistic view.

PRODUCTIVITY GROWTH

It is pertinent to note that productivity is nothing but the ability of an industry or an economy to produce goods and services with a given set of inputs. Productivity and growth in productivity, being the major determinants of level and growth of per capita income, occupy significant place in an economy. We are here interested to find the reason and factors for slow growth in productivity. Some people believe that environmental regulations are major reasons for slow productivity growth, besides other factors.

As productivity growth is taken as standard measure of progress in an economy, it is necessary to define it, before discussing its its measurement.

The productivity growth over a year is defined as the rate of growth in quality adjusted output less the rate of growth of quality adjusted inputs. The rate of growth would typically be measured in percentage terms per year. In other words, "Productivity growth is defined as the rate of growth of output less the rate of growth of inputs into production. Both inputs and out put should be measured in constant quality units. The rate of growth of inputs as a whole is a weighted average of the rates of growth of all inputs, with weights being value shares, in cost." This definition of productivity growth corresponds to multifactor or total productivity growth.

Measurement of Total Factor Productivity Growth

It is pertinent to refresh ourselves to the measurement of productivity growth, as it is affected by (sometimes/ usually as per growth economists) environmental regulations.

Consider a standard production function of the form,

$$Y = A\ f(L, K) \qquad \text{... (1)}$$

Where, Y -= Output, L = Labour, K = Capital and A = a parameter.

Let there be a small change in all variable due to a change in time, equ. (1) becomes:

$$Y + \Delta Y = [A + \Delta A)\ f\ (L + \Delta L,\ K + \Delta K) \qquad \text{...(2)}$$

After substracting Equation (1) from Equation (2), and manipulting the result, we have:

$$\Delta Y - \Delta A\ f(L,K) + MP_L.\ \Delta L. + MP_K\ \Delta K \qquad \text{... (3)}$$

Where,

MP_L and MP_K are the marginal products of labour and capital respectively.

After dividing Equ (3) by Equ (1), we get:

$$\frac{\Delta Y}{Y} = \frac{\Delta A}{A} + (LMP_L/Y)\ \Delta L/L + (KMP_K/Y)\ \Delta K/K \qquad \text{... (4)}$$

In above equation (4), the terms in parentheses are shares of each input (in value terms) on the total out put, We could expect the price f an input to be set to the value of marginal product of that input and for total cost to equal the value of output (zero profits). Thus, ($p_y.MP_L$) would be the price of labour (with p_y the price of output) and ($p_y.Y$) would be the value of output. After rewriting equation (4). We have,

$$\Delta A/A = \Delta Y/Y - \$_L\ \Delta L/L - \$_k\ \Delta K/K \qquad \text{... (14.5)}$$

Where, $\$_L = p_L\ L/(p_L\ /\ (p_L + p_K K).$

$\$_K\ p_K\ K/(p_L L + p_K K).$

The equation (5) after dividing by **t becomes

$$\frac{\Delta A}{\Delta_t A} = \frac{\Delta Y}{\Delta_t Y} - p_L \frac{\Delta_t L}{\Delta_t . L} - \$_k \frac{\Delta K}{\Delta_t K} \quad \text{... (6)}$$

$$\frac{\bar{A}}{A} = \frac{\bar{Y}}{Y} - \$_L \frac{\bar{L}}{L} - \$_k \frac{\bar{K}}{K} \quad \text{... (7)}$$

put $\frac{\Delta A}{\Delta t} = \bar{A}$, $\frac{\Delta Y}{\Delta t} = \bar{Y}$, $\frac{\Delta L}{\Delta t} = \bar{L}$ and $\frac{\Delta K}{\Delta t} = \bar{K}$ on equation (6).

Here, $\$_i$ is the value share of factor i in cost Equation (7) shows that the rate of change of A A/A) is equal to the rate of change in output less the rate of change of inputs, weighted by their relative importance (defined by value shares). A is the parameter that stands for technology. The equation (7) defines total factor or multi-factor productivity growth, because it recognises changes in both out put and all the input factors.

Single Factor Productivity Measurement

It is pertinent to note that most of the cases, measurement of productivity of one particular input is easier than the other (e.g. Labour productivity is easier to determine than of the capital). Labour productivity is often used as a simple measure of productivity growth. Labour productivity is defied as the percentage change in output less the percentage change in labour inputs.

As is clear from equation (7), if Labour and capital stay in a fixed proportions and growth the same rate, there is no loss in accuracy. In other words, if we assume

$\bar{L}/L = \bar{K}/K$, the equation (7)

$$\bar{A}/A = \bar{Y}/Y - \$_L \bar{L}/L - \$_L \frac{\bar{K}}{K}$$

$$= \bar{Y}/Y - (\$_t + \$_K)\ \bar{L}/L$$

$$= \bar{Y}/Y - \bar{L}/L \qquad \ldots (8)$$

However, Labour and capital may not grow at the same rate. It this differ, Labour productivity may be lower or higher than multi factor productivity growth.

In the case of two periods analysis, where productivity and prices of capital and labour have changed (labour is cheaper).

Owing to the price change, we would expect $\bar{K}/K = \bar{L}/L - B$, where B is some positive number. In other words, use of capital will be less or than that of labour (i.e. $\bar{K}/K < \bar{L}/L$), due to change in price. Ignoring the small changes that may occur in factor shares, Equation (7) can be written as:

$$\bar{A}/A = \bar{Y}/Y - \$_L\ \bar{L}/L - \$_K \bar{K}/K$$

$$= \bar{Y}/Y - \bar{L}/L + \$_K B. \qquad \ldots (9)$$

i.e., Total productivity growth = Labour productivity growth $\$_K B$.

As, both $\$_K$ and B are positive, a measure of labour productivity growth will understate the rate of total factor productivity growth.

Omission Bias of Environmental Factors

So far, we have not included environment, which is an input in the production of goods, in measuring the productivity growth. You can not manufacture steel without using the environment as dumping growth for pollution. Now, consider environment (E) as an input alongwith K and L, in the production of good. In case environment is cheap to use (no regulation), firms mill tend to use oa good deal of E. On the contrary, in case environment is expensive to use (light regulation or high Pigovian fee), firms would substitute other factors (such as capital) using less of E.

Notably, if we survey the past three decades, we find that the effective price of environment throughout the world has gone up dramatically. The situation of sixties, when environment could be freely used for pollution disposal, has changed drastically. To the extent environment is not considered as a factor in measures of productivity as and the price of the environment increases, measures of productivity growth will understate the extent of real productivity growth.

This is analogous to the case we just discussed in which labour productivity growth will understate multifactor productivity growth when there is a simultaneous increase in the price of nonlabour inputs (capital). Seriousness of potential understating of productivity states the error that occurs when productivity growth ignores of the inputs. Here, distortion was introduced by ignoring capital, focusing on labour productivity only. Similarly, the size of the value share of environmental inputs in total costs is an important determinant of the extent of the understatement of productivity gains. The larger the share, the greater the understatement.

Thus, industries with significant pollution or pollution control would be expected to show the greatest divergence between true productivity growth and measures that omit the environment.

It is apt to mention that various studies have tried to correct productivity measures for environmental regulations. Robert Repetto and his colleagues... have calculated multifactor productivity growth for several industries, taking into account the use of the environment as an input.

Electricity generation in particular has moved from a situation of tree use of the environment to one of strict regulation of emissions. The productivity of electric generation with environment regulation is always higher (throughout the period) than that without environmental regation. Similar is the case for agriculture. The modest increase here shows that environmental pollution is less significant to agriculture than to electricity generation. Conard and Morrison's study for Cauda, Germany. U.S.A. for period 1960-67 and 1970-80, shows interesting quantitative gains in manufacturing sectors' productivity growth due to inclusion of environmental regulation. In U.S.A., in the period 1972-80 (a period of tightening environmental regulation). The conventional and adjusted productivity growth measures were 2.2% and 2.4% of respectively. Similar, but less pronounced results were obtained for Germany and Canada.

As such it can be inferred that excluding the environment from measures of multifactor productivity growth would be expected to understate productivity growth in a period in which environemntal regulation are tightening.

Green National Accounting

Today, no one country can be single out which does not have her yearly national account—a descriction of income and expenditure item-wise. Not only this, today there is a prescribed form of standard of national accounts, which helps in comparisons across the countries.

Generally, national accounts, provides the informations about the conditions of economy. Its primary purpose is to assist policy makers in governments. Nearly all government policies that are designed to intervene in the economy rely substantially on economic data contained in the national accounts. Even ostensibly non-economic policies such as environmental regulation and funding of scientific research are influenced by data in the nation accounts. The investment in R and D can be justified by the gains to economic growth, which is the result of innovation and invention.

Environmental policy can be affected in negative way. National accounting data can show the extent to which environmental protection is retarding conventionally measured economic growth. Or, in many developing nations, significant harvesting of forests or mining of minerals is promoted on the basis of its effect on growth in GNP (it raises the growth rate, some say misleading). Although the methods of generating national accounts have evolved over the decades, they are not perfect. Several important ingradients of economic activities (like illegal activities) and economy (like environmental value) of value of environment and pollution has been significantly criticised. For instance, pumped oil from the ground is counted in GDP. But it could be argued that the inventory of all in the round is being depleted and this inventory reduction should be a substraction from GDP. Using up our oil is making the country poorer, not richer. Similar is the case of non-inclusion pollution pollution is a product like any other with two exceptions. It is not marketed and it has a negative value. If a firm produces goods worth Rs. 10,000 and creates a damage (by pollution) worth Rs. 3,000, it seem reasonable to value its total output-worth Rs. 70,000, rather than Rs. 10,000, as is currently being done in most national accounting systems.

Excluding (depletion of natural resources) is somewhat like saying that your income has gone up wen you decide to sell all the furniture in your house/your cas flow may increase but you are no richer for liquidating your assets. In the pollution case it is simpler to include.

Remarkably, today many governments are deeply interested to include environment into their national accounts and are busy to collect many details necessary for their inclusion. The *United Nations* has proposed a System of Environmental and Economic Accounting (SEEA) as a "Satellite System" to conventional system of National Accounts (SNA).

Similarly, the *United States* has proposed a "Satellite system" termed the integrated economic and environmental satellite accounts (IEESA). Thus, there is a great hope that these companion accounting system will advance in future.

Double Dividend

As is generally observed there is tradition in Governments to leavy taxes to raise its revenue. But, unfortunately, most taxes tend to introduce inefficiencies and distortions into the economy. A labour tax (wage/salary income tax) makes labour more expensive and thus discourages work. A capital tax makes capital more expensive and thus discourage investments. These inefficiencies have been empirically established by several studies, and make the statement "peny wise, pound fullish" hold. But, a conceptual shift (in this regard) is seen in recent years, when a number of proposals to substitute pollution taxes for more traditional revenue raising taxes, (as income tax), came into existence. The idea is that such taxes would not only reduce pollution but would also reduce the distortions associated with existing taxes—a "double dividend."

This policy suggestion has prompted an examination of the efficiencies of pollution taxes when there are preexisting distortions. Due to the preexisting distortionary taxes (such as income tax), pollution taxes generate an indirect cost in terms of exacerbating the preexisting inefficiencies. However, a pollution tax may off set some of this indirect inefficiencies are greater than the gains in reduced pollution damage. These are classic results in what is known as the theory of second best. What is advisable in an economy without distortions is not necessarily a good idea when there are distortions, even in apparently unrelated parts of the economy.

Also, the pollution generating commodity (x) will be produced less due to pollution tax. It the tax revenues result, then labour taxes will be reduced to keep the total government revenues constant.

Alternatively Consider the case when price of Commodity x is increased (due to taxation), the leisure will increase, to H^+. The increased quantity of leisure with respect to increase in price of x, can be computed from the *cross-price elasticity* of demand for leisure with respect to the price of good x:

$$\eta_{HL} \equiv (\Delta H / H)/(\Delta p_x / p_z) = [(H^+ - H^*)/t_x](p_x / H^*) \quad \text{... (10)}$$

Here, η_{HL} = change in demand for leisure with respect to change in price of x.

This loss must be fulfilled and every paisa that is raised through labour taxation actually costs society 1 + V. Thus, from Equ (10), the indirect loss from the environmental controls on x is,

$$IE = (1+V)\ (H^+ - H^*)\ t_L = (1+V)\ t_L t_X\ \eta_{HX}\ H^*/p_X \quad \text{... (11)}$$

Where, IE = 'Tax interact Effect.' which is positive remember that it is a los.

V = marginal dead weight loss.

As such, the tax interaction effect is the extra inefficiency from a pollution regulation due to the fact that labour is already taxed. Remember that there will be no tx interaction effect when there is not tax on labour, (i.e. $t_L = 0$). Furthermore, the greater -the volume of n_{HX} the larger of effect.

Basically, the pollution tax is producing a deadweight loss by marginally changing the very significant pre-existing deadweight loss associated with labour taxation.

Although IE is unequivocally a welfare loss (provided the good is substitute for leisure), there are two welfare gains from pollution regulation:

One, is the reduction in damage associated with the pollution. Less pollution means less damage (term this as Pigovian Effect, PE).

Remember here that RE is zero in case of no revenue raise/increase through the environmental regulation.

In case of command and control regulation, no revenue is raised, where as it raises in the marketable permits for pollution regulation. In case permits are given away initially then RE = 0.

In the last, but not the least, we conventionally believe/think that the Pigovian Effect (PE) is the primary gain from a pollution control regulations. It has already been found that if pollution tax revenues can be used to reduce distortionary taxes, we have a bonus of the recycling effect (RE). But it is also seen that reduction in pollution generates a loss through the indirect effect on pre-existing distortionary taxes (IE). This raises tax-interaction effect. The emirical evidences are available in Parry (1995), Goulder et al. (1991) and many other's studies.

However, it might seem unfair that environment bear the cost of the inefficiency introduced by the wage tax. But it is incorrect interpretation of the result. In fact, in this type of second-best environment, it is difficult to interpret what is happening with the emission tax without looking at the distortions through out the economy introduced by the income tax.

For example, if the polluting good and leisure are substitutes as assumed, the subsidy to leisure may as assumed, the subsidy to leisure may already have reduced consumption of the polluting good in the economy. Thus, there is no need to reduce it as much with the emissions tax. In fact it has been shown that when there are no commoditily taxes and an optimal income tax, it can be welfare improving to subsidize the consumption of goods that are substitutes for leisure.

Although, no assumption, that the income tax is optimal, is made, if it were and there were no tax or subsidy on the polluting good, the optimal action would be to simultaneously tax the polluting good at the full marginal damage but then add a subsidy to account for distortions of the income tax. The net effect is that the tax on the polluting good is less than marginal damage done by it.

REFERENCES

C.D. Kolstad, *Env. Economics* fn. 18, p. 287.

Christiansen, V., "Which commodity tax should supplement the Income Tax?", *J. Public Eco.* 24: 195-220 (1994).

Conard, K. and C. Morrison, "The Impact of Pollution Abatement Investment on Productivity change: An Empirical comparison of the U.S., Germany and Canada," *South Econ.* J, 55: 684-697 (1989).

Gouler, L.H., I.W.H. Parry, and D. Burtraw, "Revenue Raising Versus Other Approaches to Environmental Protection: The critical

Significance of Pre-existing Tax distortions," *Rand J. ECO* 28:708-731 (1997).

Parry, I.W.H, "Pollution Taxes and Revenue Recycling," J. *Envir.Eco.Mgmt.,* 29 (No. 2, Part 2), S: 64 - S-77 (1995).

Repetto, R., D. Rothman, P. Faeth and D. Austin, "Has Environmental Protection Really Reduced Productivity Growth," (World Resources Institute, Washington, D.C., Oct. 1996).

Squitres, D., "Productivity Measurement in Common Property Resource Industries, An Application to the Pacific coast Trawl Fishery," *Rand J. Econ,* 23:221-236 (1992).

United States Department of Commerce (1994.a).

7

Hedonic Value Method

> "Those who believe we have reached the limit of business progress and employment opportunity in this country are like the farmer who had two windmills and pulled one down because he was afraid there was not enough wind for both."
>
> —*Morris S. Tremaine*

The very word "Hedonic" is derived from the Greek word "Hedone", which means "pleasure." Thus, hedonic value implies pleasure giving value or prices. In this way, the methods which provides the pleasure value/price of property (or, environmental goods and services) is the content of his chapter. Here, we are concerned with revealed preference. method of inferring demand for environmental goods and services. Thus, we shall concentrate on drawing the inference by observing markets which are closely related to the pollution or other environmental good. For example, the risk contents in some job is greater than the other and the wages for risky job is also greater in comparison of the non-risk job. This tell us about how people value risk differences. On the same line the difference the value of property in a non-air polluted city and air polluted city, shows the valuation of clean air by the people.

The primary empirical approach (quantification approach) which measures (or value/or give price) is known as hedonic price (value) method. This can best be explained through examples. Note the price of houses for different levels, of air pollution in a city or region and now study the changes in the price in response to the changes in air pollution, keeping everything else constant. Similarly, one can measure how wages change with the risk, and then draw the inference that would be induced in wages from a small change in risk. In either case, one begins with an hedonic price function that gives the price of house or the wage as a function of air pollution or risk as well as other variables. Once this relationship is quantified, the next step would be to infer/find out the marginal value of a change in the air pollution or risk variable.

Now, we will attempt to consider at the general problem of relating pollution levels to property values, ignoring the labour market. Afterward, a generalisation of this will be used to analyse the effect of pollution on property values and wages in the case of mobile producers and labours.

- In an agricultural region, the value of a change in air pollution in an area which constitutes a small part of the agricultural market will be reflected in the change in the land price.
- In case, a substantial amount of land is affected by change in air pollution, so that prices of agricultural products changes, land price changes will not reflect the value of the change in air pollution
- In an urban housing market, in case of a closed market where migration in and out are restricted, the value of pollution changes will not be fully reflected in land value changes. On the other hand, in case of open market (region) with free mobility in and out of the region, the value of changes in air pollution in a part of the market will be reflected improperly value. Here producers are unaffected by the change in pollution and property values.

- A change in pollution will change both property values and wages, when production is affected by pollution or property values are significant costs of production. In case of pollution being "productive," firms' costs are reduced, and increases in pollution will raise wages and have ambiguous impact on land price.

  On the contrary, in case of pollution being "improductive," pollution increases production costs, an increase in pollution will diminish land price and have an ambiguous fact on wages.

  But, in case of pollution being "neutral" to the firm, increase in pollution decreases land prices and increases wages, although the amount of each depends on the relative importance of land and labor to production.

- With hedonic price theory, one observes the price of a good as a function of certain characteristics of the good. From this, one finds the marginal price of the characteristic as the slope of the price line with respect the characteristic.

- Hedonic price can also be used to estimate the individual's demand curve. Not only this, after observation, one can estimate the marginal willingness to pay for the characteristic by using marginal price of the characteristic for consumers.

- In studies of wage-risk trade-off, the marginal wage with respect to fatality risk has been called the value of statistical life. The VLS is the ratio of increased wage rate to the increase of fatality that induced the increase in wages.

Rent of Land and Pollution

It is pertinent to note that the price of a land price is determined by many factors. On first place, it is the value of the stream of services that the land price can be *expected* to provide in the future, netted back to the present. The *expected* word clearly indicates about the uncertainty in the value of land because of the ambiguity of the future usefulness of the land piece. This becomes the major cause of fluctuations of land prices in future. As expectations can not be observed it becomes pertinent to distinguish the rental price and asset price of the land. Rental price of land is the price at which the land is given to some one for a short period of time (e.g. a year or so). There is no role or little role of expectation in rental price. It is totally related to the lead's value during the rental period. On the contrary. The asset price of land is the price of taking title to the land in perpetuity. Its value may increases today on the expectation of its usefulness in future. Agricultural land near a city may be used for housing in future. This will increase the asset price of the land today.

Secondly, the price of the land also depends on the situation and productivity of the land. If the land is being used for agricultural purposes, the rental value of the land in a particular year is the expected value of output from the land, less the cost of labour, seed, irrigation and other non land inputs, required/used to get the out put. The productive efficiency of land/quality of land sever air pollution, salination, etc., are major determinants of its productivity. The rental value of the land is decided on the expected value of yield from that land.

The rental value of land also depends on the purpose it is being used, is situation and its locational surroundings, etc. For example, a land being used for housing, situated in pleasant surroundings easily accessible, may fetch greater value. The land in the centre of a metropolitan city is more costly (rental value) than in the vicinity of desert or hazardous situation.

The urban land valuation depends on the supply and demand of land for building, not on its agricultural productivity. According to Edwin S. Mills, 'The classic economic model of a city consists of a downtown in which every one works, surrounded by concentric rings of housing. In each ring, the price of land is the same since the commuting time (to the city centre) is constant. Rings that are further from the centre, have lower land prices since commuting times are longer. Far from the centre, the price of land drops so much that agriculture is a better use of the land than housing. This determines the extent of the City.

The locational variation in air pollution raises some basis issues. Is it possible to infer anything from the land value differences that might be induced by these variations in pollution levels? Can one assume that all the land price difference between the higher land prices in clear air areas compare to lower land prices in dirty air areas is due to the difference in pollution levels? The problem is not so simple. Hence, we will study this problem according to the use value (or use) of land one-by-one.

As, wages do not very from an area high pollution to an areas of less pollutin in an region, we will assume that wages are unaffected by pollution for analysing/focussing on the effects we will explicitly introduce wages in addition to land rents and analyse the responses of both these to differences in pollution. levels. But for a short while, we assume wages are exogenous.

1. Agricultural Land, Pollution and Rent Value

Let us consider a vast land area devoted to agricultural production. Now make a division of this area into two regions—a clean region and a dirty region. Due to the pollution, productivity in the dirty region is low. Because of the lower productivity rental price of the land is also low compare to the clean region renal price. We would expect the difference in value between the two regions to reflect the difference in productivity of the land in the two regions due to air pollution, since everything else is the same.

Now, the fundamental question here arises as, how much dirty region's land-owners would be willing to pay to clean up the pollution in dirty region? Is it exactly the same amount that land prices are depressed in the dirty region? It this is so, we just observe the land price differential and we have a measure of the willingness to pay for clean air. The authenticity of this will depend on the nature of the agricultural markets for the produce grown on the land. In case of local market, the price of the agricultural out put from the region will be determined locally. The increase in supply of crop due to cleaning up the pollution, will/may reduce the crop price, in both the dirty and the clean area. This results in the land price in the clean area, in conjunction with an increase in the land prices in the dirty area. Both, producers (landowners) as well as consumers will benefit from cleaner air. Thus, the land value change will not fully capture the value of the cleaner air.

In contrast, owing to nature of market of many crops being regional (not national or global), the clean-up of local air pollution will not affect the price of the product. This implies in no change in land price in clean area because of elimination of pollution from the dirty area. In this case, the land value change is reasonable proxy for the value to agriculture of the environmental improvement.

2. Urban Land Value and Pollution

In case of urban land, which is used for residence (housing), the value of land reflects the utility of the people residing on the land rather than the value of agricultural products produced the land. Now again consider two part of land in a city. The first part suffers from pollution of air (dirty) and the second part is clean. It is assumed that for air pollution, everything (surroundings, neighbourhood, commuting time etc.) are same in both clean an dirty region. Also, it is assumed that everyone in the city is the same, both in terms of their preferences and in terms of their incomes. Again we face the same question as in the case of agricultural land example: Does the lower value of the property in the dirty region fully capture the damage from the air pollution?

This can be explained by taking two types of cities "closed city" and "open city". The migration in-or-out is assumed to be absent and thus population remains fixed (stable) in closed city. On the contrary, the migration in-or-out is assumed to be present and the mobility among cities is costless in open city. People can move easily to better utility yielding cities free of cost, bidding up prices and depressing attainable utility until the utility differential is erased/vanished. The same applies for different locations within a city. This means that the utility of the people living dirty part and clean part, is the same, otherwise, they would not put up with the dirty air. To compensate for the pollution, living is cheaper. Now, after cleaning up the pollution, there will be increase in the value of the land. This may be beneficial for landowners only. This is because the utility level is the same over all of the cities and a clean up in one part of one city will not significantly change the overall level of utility.

Thus, with the air becaming cleaner, the land value will rise to compensate exactly for the increased quality of life. In other words, the increased value of land is a perfect measure of the value of the air quantity improvement. Of course, if we relax our assumption of homogeneity, and in fact consider a homogenous population (different tastes, different labour skills, different incomes), this conclusion must be tempered. However, the interplay between wages and property values, will be the subject matter of next section analysis.

In the case of closed city, the utility level of the typical citizen is determined by internal factors, only. One is not aware of the utility level within the city is the same for all the residents. Thus, the difference in property values between the clean and dirty parts of the city reflects the damage from air pollution. Now in case the pollution is eliminated, will the rise in properly values in the dirty area reflect the value of the cleaner air? Emphatically N. The reason is that the utility level of the typical resident of the city will rise as well as property values. There are two effects of pollution elimination — one observable (property value in crease) and two unobservable, (utility level increases).

Conclusion

From the above discussion one can conclude that in some but not all cases, the value of improving environmental quantity will be reflected in increased property values. It will not hold in the situations involving secondary changes in utility or economic surplus brought about by the improved environmental quality, and not reflected in property values. This could be an increase in consumer surplus from lower agricultural prices or an increase in overall well-being brought about by the improvement and not bid away through higher land prices.

RELATIONSHIP BETWEEN POLLUTION, LAND PRICES AND WAGES

An attempt is already made to examine the extent to which various environmental and other reasons causing differentials, are reflected in properly values. There are places in this world, which are not environmentally congineal to live, but have higher land/property values e.g. p central places in a cosmopolitan city. On the other hand, there are many such places where quality of environment is very high, but value of land is very low, e.g. places in villages or near hills.

Also, wages in city compare to rural areas are higher can we conclude that rise in wages is the compensation for environmental quality deterioration? This clearly suggests to consider wages differences as well as property value differences in under standing the value of change in environmental quality.

In fact, the fundamental curiosity in environmentalists as well as economists is to know the extent of levels of pollution which depress the property values but enhances wages to compensate for the pollution. A simple model involving multiple cities, which are in competition for firms and residents, will easily explain the interplay among pollution levels, property values, and wages. One can expect differences in wages and/or property values in the case when pollution levels are different in the different cities.

Nordhaus Model : Effect of Climate on Wages and Rents

Nordhaus (1996) examines the effect of climate change on wages and rents. William Nordhaus in his article "Climate Amenities and Global Warming" tries to establish the extent to which the amenity value of climate to individual is reflected in wages and property values. This value is a final demand value, not related to production in any way. For this study, Nordhaus examined some 3000 counties in United States with this expectation that there will be variation in wages and land prices from county to county and that the price of treated goods would be equalised. Taking climate as sunshine, he developed a possible (more is better, wages, and housing prices.

This relationship is consistent with sunshine being neutral in production. More sunshine is desirable and thus drives down wages and drives up land prices. For higher level of sunshines, wages (nominal wages) fall while housing prices rise. Note that Nordhaus, avoid dealing with change in two variables (housing prices and wages) by adjusting wages by the cost of living (including housing cost). In this way he departs from the framework of our model in the previous sections. He calls the adjusted wages as real wages. Due to higher housing cost, consumer will be left little income for consumption purposes.

Real wages drops in response to increase in index of sunshines. For instance, if A's income is Rs. 1000, and B's income is Rs. 5000, but the cost of living for A is twice what it is for B. Then the real wages for A and B will be same. Now, a cam buy a commodity in Rs. 2, while B can be the same commodity in Rs 1. This adjustment made it possible to show the changes in real wages with climate.

Nordhaus proposed, through his model, to develop a relationship between real wages (wr), climate variables and other factors, which determine the real wages such as educational level of population). The proposed model takes the following from:

$$W_r = \alpha_o - \alpha_c C + \alpha_z Z + e$$

Where, w_r represents real wages,

C represents climate,

Z represents non-climate factors,

e error terms

and α_o, α_x and α_z represents corresponding parameters.

Here,

(i) climate includes many variables, such as mean

annual temperature, summer temperature, precipitation etc.

(ii) Non-climate variables (z) includes the variables that are thought to determine wages (e.g., density of population, educational level, ethnic background, unemployment, rates etc.

(iii) Number of observations are 3000 taken from a cross selection of U.S. countries.

The significance of Nordhaus study lies in exploring the relationship of different levels of environmental good with wages and housing costs. How the farmer influences the letter two. Unfortunately, seeing how environmental good influences equilibrium prices in not generally enough for us to compute demand for the environmental good. To do that, more structures are required.

HEDONIC PRICE THEORY

In "real world" one is often confronted with bundle (bunch) of goods with a single price for the while bunch. Even then, he is interested in the price of an element of the bunch. For example, different occupations (jobs) possess different characteristic, including level of health or mortality or disability risk. Typically, higher wages are paid for the higher risk jobs. Is it possible to draw some inference, after observing the wages associated with many different jobs, *about the workers valuation for small changes in risks?* We can take example of prices of houses which possesses good number of rooms, neighbourhood quality, and surrounding environmental quality.

It was observed that the prices of houses with fewer rooms or houses with poor air quality are comparatively lower. By observe the prices of several houses having different characteristics, is it possible to back out the implicit value that is being placed on air quality (for instance)?

These examples suggest the focus of hedonic price theory: inferring the value placed on characteristics of goods based on the observed price of a bundle of goods. It is some what more complicated that these examples suggest, in part because of the interaction between the supply of characteristics (building more houses with more rooms) and the demand for characteristics.

For the determination of the price of good in the market and inferring about consumers' willingness to pay for changes in the characteristic—a demand curve, we would assume/consider the simplest possible structure of the good with a single characteristic for instance, a house with few number of rooms or pollution level, may be considered, which may later on implied for multiple characteristics.

From the view point of the good (a house), a city or part of a city, may be considered as a single homogeneous area. Air quality level is assumed as single variable (z) (characteristics) of every house. Now, our concern is to know/analyse the variation in the prices of a house with the pollution level. In other words, we are interested in p(z), the price of house as a function of air quality levels. The price function is an equilibrium concept, resulting from the interaction of supply and demand. From this a single house price for every pollution level is obtained.

Assumptions of Hedonic Price Theory

1. There is competition in the market.
2. Production take p(z) (i.e. price) as given.
3. Consumer take p(z) (i.e. price) as given (It is like conventional competitive market where price "p" is given for both the consumers as well as producers).
4. The good produced in which lies in the single homogenous area.

The way consumers and producers react to p(z) will provide us insight into how p(z) in the market. The market equilibrium depends on the demand (consumer side) and supply (producer side) of the good.

Having a thorough understanding of hedonic value method in environmental economics in the preceding discussion, now we will put light on environmental accounting in the next chapter.

REFERENCES

C.D. Kolstad, *Env. Eco.,* p. 335, Notes No. 12.

Mendelsohn, Robert, William D. Nordhaus, and Diagee Shaw, "The Impact of Global Warming on Agriculture: A Ricardian Study." *Am. Eco. Rev.,* 84:753-771 (1994).

Mills Edwins. S., "An Aggregative Model of Resource Allocation in a Metropolitan Areas", *Am. Eco. Rev.,* Papers Proc., 57(2): 197-210 (1967).

Nordhaus, William D., "Climate Amenities and Global Warming," in N. Nakicenovic, W.D. Nordhaus, R. Richels, and F.C. Toth (Eds.), Climate Change: Integrating Science, Economics and Policy, Proceedings of Confer at IIASA, Luxeumburg, Austria. IIASA Report C.P.-96-1 (Dec. 1996).

Polinsky and Shavell (1976) for an analysis of a more general urban area.

Ridker and Henning (1967), 'The Determinants of Residential Property Values with Special Reference to Air Pollution; Rev, Econ. Stat, 49: 246-257 (1967).

Roback, Jenifer, "Wages, Rents and Quality of Life," *J. Political Eco.,* 90:1257-1278 (1982).

8

Environmental Accounting

Sustainability measurement is a term that denotes the measurements used as the quantitative basis for the informed management of sustainability. The metrics used for the measurement of sustainability (involving the sustainability of environmental, social and economic domains, both individually and in various combinations) are still evolving: they include indicators, benchmarks, audits, indexes and accounting, as well as assessment, appraisal and other reporting systems. They are applied over a wide range of spatial and temporal scales.

Some of the best known and most widely used sustainability measures include corporate sustainability reporting, Triple Bottom Line accounting, and estimates of the quality of sustainability governance for individual countries using the Environmental Sustainability Index and Environmental Performance Index.

The principal objective of sustainability indicators is to inform public policy-making as part of the process of sustainability governance. Sustainability indicators can provide information on any aspect of the interplay between the environment and socio-economic activities. Building strategic indicator sets generally deals with just a few simple questions: what is happening? (descriptive indicators), does it matter and are we reaching targets? (performance indicators), are we improving? (efficiency indicators), are measures working? (policy effectiveness indicators), and are we generally better off? (total welfare indicators). One popular general framework used by The European Environment Agency uses a slight modification of the Organisation for Economic Cooperation and Development DPSIR system. This breaks up environmental impact into five stages. Social and economic developments (consumption and production) *(D)rive* or initiate environmental *(P)ressures* which, in turn, produces a change in the *(S)tate* of the environment which leads to *(I)mpacts* of various kinds. Societal *(R)esponses* (policy guided by sustainability indicators) can be introduced at any stage of this sequence of events.

The United Nations has developed extensive sustainability measurement tools in relation to sustainable development as well as a System of Integrated Environmental and Economic Accounting.

In the last couple of decades there has arisen a crowded toolbox of quantitative methods used to assess sustainability — including measures of resource use like life cycle assessment, measures of consumption like the ecological footprint and measurements of quality of environmental governance like the Environmental Performance Index. The following is a list of quantitative "tools" used by sustainability scientists - the different categories are for convenience only as defining criteria will intergrade. It would be too difficult to list all those methods available at different levels of organisation so those listed here are at for the global level only.

This list is incomplete; you can help by expanding it.

- Benchmarks

A benchmark is a point of reference for a measurement. Once a benchmark is established it is possible to assess trends and measure progress. Baseline global data on a range of sustainability parameters is available at list of global sustainability statistics.

- Indexes

  A sustainability index is an aggregate sustainability indicator that combines multiple sources of data. There is a *Consultative Group on Sustainable Development Indices*

- Quality Index
- Child Development Index
- Corruption Perceptions Index
- Democracy Index
- Environmental Performance Index
- Emergy Sustainability Index
- Education Index
- Environmental Sustainability Index
- Environmental Vulnerability Index
- GDP per capita
- Gini coefficient
- Gender Parity Index
- Gender-related Development Index
- Gender Empowerment Measure
- Gross national happiness
- Genuine Progress Indicator
- (formerly Index of Sustainable Economic Welfare)
- Gross National Product
- Happy Planet Index

- Human Development Index (see List of countries by HDI)
- Legatum Prosperity Index
- Index of Sustainable Economic Welfare
- Life Expectancy Index

Sustainable Governance Indicators. The Status Index ranks 30 OECD countries in terms of sustainable reform performance

Sustainable Society Index: Water Poverty Index

- metrics

  Many environmental problems ultimately relate to the human effect on those global biogeochemical cycles that are critical to life. Over the last decade monitoring these cycles has become a more urgent target for research:

- water cycle
- carbon cycle
- phosphorus cycle
- nitrogen cycle
- sulphur cycle
- oxygen cycle
- auditing

Sustainability auditing and reporting are used to evaluate the sustainability performance of a company, organization, or other entity using various performance indicators. Popular auditing procedures available at the global level include:

- ISO 14000
- ISO 14031
- Natural Step

- Triple Bottom Line Accounting
- input-output analysis can be used for any level of organization with a financial budget. It relates environmental impact to expenditure by calculating the resource intensity of goods and services.
- development and NGO project auditing
  "Litmus test" type indicators are also used in the development and NGO community to test conformity and compliance with the guidelines of sustainable human development and the international Rio Declaration of 1992.
- Sustainable development indicator for NGOs and Other Organizations
- reporting
  - o Global Reporting Initiative Global Reporting Initiative modelling and monitoring procedures. Many of these have only just been developed.
  - o State of the Environment reporting provides general background information on the environment and is progressively including more indicators.
  - o European sustainability
- accounting
  Some accounting methods attempt to include environmental costs rather than treating them as externalities
- Green accounting
- Sustainable Value
- Sustainability economics

Resource Metrics

Part of this process can relate to resource use such as

energy accounting or to economic metrics or price system values as compared to non-market economics potential, for understanding resource use. An important task for resource theory (energy economics) is to develop methods to optimize resource conversion processes. These systems are described and analyzed by means of the methods of mathematics and the natural sciences. Human factors, however, have dominated the development of our perspective of the relationship between nature and society since at least the Industrial Revolution, and in particular have influenced how we describe and measure the economic impacts of changes in resource quality. A balanced view of these issues requires an understanding of the physical framework in which all human ideas, institutions, and aspirations must operate.

Economics, Oil and Energy

When oil production first began in the mid-nineteenth century, the largest oil fields recovered fifty barrels of oil for every barrel used in the extraction, transportation and refining. This ratio is often referred to as the Energy Return on Energy Investment (EROI or EROEI). Currently, between one and five barrels of oil are recovered for each barrel-equivalent of energy used in the recovery process. As the EROEI drops to one, or equivalently the Net energy gain falls to zero, the oil production is no longer a net energy source. This happens long before the resource is physically exhausted.

Note that it is important to understand the distinction between a barrel of oil, which is a measure of oil, and a barrel of oil equivalent (BOE), which is a measure of energy. Many sources of energy, such as fission, solar, wind, and coal, are not subject to the same near-term supply restrictions that oil is. Accordingly, even an oil source with an EROEI of 0.5 can be usefully exploited if the energy required to produce that oil comes from a cheap and plentiful energy source. Availability of cheap, but hard to transport, natural gas in some oil fields has led to using natural gas to fuel enhanced oil recovery. Similarly, natural gas in huge amounts is used to power most Athabasca Tar Sands plants. Cheap natural gas has also led to Ethanol fuel produced with a net EROEI of less than 1, although figures in this area are controversial because methods to measure EROEI are in debate.

Insofar as economic growth is driven by oil consumption growth, post-peak societies must adapt. M. King Hubbert believed:

> "Our principal constraints are cultural. During the last two centuries we have known nothing but exponential growth and in parallel we have evolved what amounts to an exponential-growth culture, a culture so heavily dependent upon the continuance of exponential growth for its stability that it is incapable of reckoning with problems of nongrowth."

Some economists describe the problem as uneconomic growth or a false economy. At the political right, Fred Ikle has warned about "conservatives addicted to the Utopia of Perpetual Growth". Brief oil interruptions in 1973 and 1979 markedly slowed - but did not stop - the growth of world GDP.

Between 1950 and 1984, as the Green Revolution transformed agriculture around the globe, world grain production increased by 250%. The energy for the Green Revolution was provided by fossil fuels in the form of fertilizers (natural gas), pesticides (oil), and hydrocarbon fueled irrigation.

David Pimentel, professor of ecology and agriculture at Cornell University, and Mario Giampietro, senior researcher at the National Research Institute on Food and

Nutrition (INRAN), place in their study *Food, Land, Population and the U.S. Economy* the maximum U.S. population for a sustainable economy at 200 million. To achieve a sustainable economy world population will have to be reduced by two-thirds, says the study. Without population reduction, this study predicts an agricultural crisis beginning in 2020, becoming critical c. 2050. The peaking of global oil along with the decline in regional natural gas production may precipitate this agricultural crisis sooner than generally expected. Dale Allen Pfeiffer claims that coming decades could see spiraling food prices without relief and massive starvation on a global level such as never experienced before.

Although Hubbert peak theory receives most attention in relation to peak oil production, it has also been applied to other natural resources.

Doug Reynolds predicted in 2005 that the North American peak would occur in 2007. Bentley (p. 189) predicted a world "decline in conventional gas production from about 2020".

Peak coal is significantly further out than peak oil, but we can observe the example of anthracite in the USA, a high grade coal whose production peaked in the 1920s. Anthracite was studied by Hubbert, and matches a curve closely. Pennsylvania's coal production also matches Hubbert's curve closely, but this does not mean that coal in Pennsylvania is exhausted—far from it. If production in Pennsylvania returned at its all time high, there are reserves for 190 years. Hubbert had recoverable coal reserves worldwide at 2500 × 10^9 metric tons and peaking around 2150(depending on usage).

More recent estimates suggest an earlier peak. *Coal: Resources and Future Production* (PDF 630KB), published on April 5, 2007 by the Energy Watch Group (EWG), which reports to the German Parliament, found that global coal production could peak in as few as 15 years. Reporting on this Richard Heinberg also notes that the date of peak annual energetic extraction from coal will likely come earlier than the date of peak in quantity of coal (tons per year) extracted as the most energy-dense types of coal have been mined most extensively. A second study, *The Future of Coal* by B. Kavalov and S. D. Peteves of the Institute for Energy (IFE), prepared for European Commission Joint Research Centre, reaches similar conclusions and states that “”coal might not be so abundant, widely available and reliable as an energy source in the future”.

Work by David Rutledge of Caltech predicts that the total of world coal production will amount to only about 450 gigatonnes. This implies that coal is running out faster than usually assumed.

Finally, insofar as global peak oil and peak in natural gas are expected anywhere from imminently to within decades at most, any increase in coal production (mining) per annum to compensate for declines in oil or NG production, would necessarily translate to an earlier date of peak as compared with peak coal under a scenario in which annual production remains constant.

In a paper in 1956, after a review of US fissionable reserves, Hubbert notes of nuclear power:

> “There is promise, however, provided mankind can solve its international problems and not destroy itself with nuclear weapons, and provided world population (which is now expanding at such a rate as to double in less than a century) can somehow be brought under control, that we may at last have found an energy supply adequate for our needs for at least the next few centuries of the “foreseeable future.”

Technologies such as the thorium fuel cycle, reprocessing and fast breeders can, in theory, considerably extend the life of uranium reserves. Roscoe Bartlett claims

> "Our current throwaway nuclear cycle uses up the world reserve of low-cost uranium in about 20 years."

Caltech physics professor David Goodstein has stated that

> "... you would have to build 10,000 of the largest power plants that are feasible by engineering standards in order to replace the 10 terawatts of fossil fuel we're burning today ... that's a staggering amount and if you did that, the known reserves of uranium would last for 10 to 20 years at that burn rate. So, it's at best a bridging technology ... You can use the rest of the uranium to breed plutonium 239 then we'd have at least 100 times as much fuel to use. But that means you're making plutonium, which is an extremely dangerous thing to do in the dangerous world that we live in."

Hubbert applied his theory to "rock containing an abnormally high concentration of a given metal" and reasoned that the peak production for metals such as copper, tin, lead, zinc and others would occur in the time frame of decades and iron in the time frame of two centuries like coal. The price of copper rose 500% between 2003 and 2007 was by some attributed to peak copper. Copper prices later fell, along with many other commodities and stock prices, as demand shrank from fear of a global recession. Lithium availability is a concern for a fleet of Li-ion battery using cars but a paper published in 1996 estimated that world reserves are adequate for at least 50 years. A similar prediction for platinum use in fuel cells notes that the metal could be easily recycled.

Phosphorus supplies are essential to farming and depletion of reserves is estimated at somewhere from 60 to 130 years. Individual countries supplies vary widely; without a recycling initiative America's supply is estimated around 30 years. Phosphorus supplies affect total agricultural output which in turn limits alternative fuels such as biodiesel and ethanol.

Hubbert's original analysis did not apply to renewable resources. However over-exploitation often results in a Hubbert peak nonetheless. A modified Hubbert curve applies to any resource that can be harvested faster than it can be replaced.

For example, a reserve such as the Ogallala Aquifer can be mined at a rate that far exceeds replenishment. This turns much of the world's underground water and lakes into finite resources with peak usage debates similar to oil. These debates usually center around agriculture and suburban water usage but generation of electricity from nuclear energy or coal and tar sands mining mentioned above is also water resource intensive. The term fossil water is sometimes used to describe aquifers whose water is not being recharged.

Renewable Resources

Fisheries: At least one researcher has attempted to perform Hubbert linearization (Hubbert curve) on the whaling industry, as well as charting the transparently dependent price of caviar on sturgeon depletion. Another example is the cod of the North Sea. The comparison of the cases of fisheries and of mineral extraction tells us that the human pressure on the environment is causing a wide range of resources to go through a depletion cycle which follows a Hubbert curve.

After having a look at environmental accounting in this chapter, now we will come to environmental tariff in the next chapter.

[Source: ***Wikipedia*****]**

REFERENCES

Bell, Simon and Morse, Stephen 2008. *Sustainability Indicators. Measuring the Immeasurable?* 2nd edn. London: Earthscan.

Boulanger, P. M. (2008) "Sustainable development indicators: a scientific challenge, a democratic issue". *S.A.P.I.EN.S.* 1 (1)

Consultative Group on Sustainable Development Indices. International Institute for Sustainable Development.

Dalal-Clayton, Barry and Sadler, Barry 2009. *Sustainability Appraisal. A Sourcebook and Reference Guide to International Experience.* London: Earthscan.

EUROSTAT. (2007). "Measuring progress towards a more sustainable Europe. 2007 monitoring report of the EU sustainable development strategy." Retrieved on 2009-04-14.

Global Reporting Initiative Guidelines 2002. http://www.epeat.net/Docs/GRI_guidelines.pdf. Retrieved 2008-06-18.

Global Reporting Initiative. Global Reporting Initiative. http://www.globalreporting.org/Home. Retrieved 2008-06-18.

Hak, T., Moldan, B. & Dahl, A.L. 2007. SCOPE 67. *Sustainability indicators.* Island Press, London.

Hill, J. 1992. *Towards Good Environmental Practice.* The Institute of Business Ethics, London.

International Corporate Sustainability Reporting. http://www.enviroreporting.com/detail_page.phtml?page=resource2.

Stanners, D. et al. 2007. *Frameworks for environmental assessment and indicators at the EEA.* In: Hak, T., Moldan, B. & Dahl, A.L. 2007. SCOPE 67. *Sustainability indicators.* Island Press, London.

Sullivan, C.A. et al. (eds) 2003. The water poverty index: development and application at the community scale. *Natural Resources Forum* 27: 189-199.

Sustainability Accounting in UK Local Government. The Association of Chartered Certified Accountants.

9

Environmental Tariff

An Environmental tariff, also known as a green tariff or eco-tariff, is an import or export tax placed on products being imported from, or also being sent to countries with substandard environmental pollution controls. They can be used as controls on global pollution and can also be considered as corrective measures against "environmental races to the bottom" and "eco-dumping".

There has been debate on the role that increased international trade has played in increasing pollution. While some maintain that increases in pollution which result in both local environmental degradation and a global *tragedy of the commons* are intimately linked to increases in international trade, others have argued that as citizens become more affluent they'll also advocate for cleaner environments.

According to a World Bank paper:

> "Since freer trade raises income, it directly contributes to increasing pollution levels via the scale effect. However, it thereby induces the composition (and) technique effects of increased income, both of which tend to reduce pollution levels".

Early Tariff Implementation Proposal

Although the United States has in the past been accused

of dragging its feet on implementing tough new anti-pollution measures, it was the originator of a legislative proposal suggesting an environmental tariff be applied against exporting countries whose exports gained significant cost advantages due to less stringent environmental regulations. The proposed legislation was tabled as the International Pollution Deterrence Act of 1991 and was introduced in its Senate in April of that year.

A notable feature of the proposed U.S. *International Pollution Deterrence Act* was the international pollution control index it cited within its Section 5, which read:

International Pollution Control Index

Section 8002 of the Solid Waste Disposal Act (42 U.S.C. 6982) is amended by adding the following new subsections at the end thereof:

> '(t) The Administrator shall prepare, within one hundred and twenty days of the enactment of this section and yearly thereafter, a pollution control index for each of the top fifty countries identified by the Office of Trade and Investment of the Department of Commerce based on the value of exports to the United States from that country's attainment of pollution control standards in the areas of air, water, hazardous waste and solid waste as compared to the United States. The purpose of this index is to measure the level of compliance within each country with standards comparable to or greater than those in the United States. The Administrator shall analyze, in particular, the level of technology employed and actual costs incurred for pollution control in the major export sectors of each country in formulating the index.

Environment tariffs were not implemented in the past, in part, because they were not sanctioned by multilateral trade regimes such as the World Trade Organization and within the General Agreement on Tariffs and Trade (GATT), a fact which generated considerable criticism and calls for reform. Additionally, many newly industrialized countries and underdeveloped countries saw the attempts to impose pollution controls on them as suspicious...

> "...seeing it as a threat to their growth and fearing that developed countries would attempt to export their preferences for pollution control or to place 'environmental' tariffs on imports from countries with lower standards."

REFERENCES

Dean, Judith M & Lovely, Mary E (2008), *Trade Growth, Production Fragmentation, and China's Environment*, Pgs. 3 & 5, National Bureau of Economic Research, Working Paper 13860, Cambridge, MA

Horvath, John Salami Tactics, Telepolis, at Heise.de online, 2000. Retrieved 2009-10-14.

International Pollution Deterrence Act of 1991 (Introduced in Senate) U.S. Congress Thomas online database, 102nd Congress, 1st session, 25 April 1991.

International Trade and Climate Change: Economic, Legal, and Institutional Perspectives Pg. 36, World Bank Publications, 2007.

International Trade and Climate Change: Economic, Legal, and Institutional Perspectives, World Bank Publications, 2007.

Jean-Marie, Grether & Mathys, Nicole A. & Jaime, de Melo, 2006, *Unraveling the World-Wide Pollution Haven Effect*, Universite de Lausanne, Ecole des HEC, DEEP - Cahiers de Recherches Economiques du Département d'Econometrie et d'Economie politique (DEEP).

Kraus, Christiane (2000), *Import Tariffs as Environmental Policy Instruments*, Springer.

Leonard, Jeffrey H., 1988, *Pollution and the Struggle for the World Product: Multinational Corporations, Environment, and International Comparative Advantage* Pg. 69, Cambridge University Press.

Mani, Muthukumara S., 1966, *Environmental Tariffs on Polluting Imports: An Empirical Study*, , Environmental & Resource Economics, European Association of Environmental and

Resource Economists, Volume 7 Issue 4 (June 1996), Pgs. 391-411.

Robison, David H., 1988, *Industrial Pollution Abatement: The Impact on Balance of Trad*, Canadian Journal of Economics, Canadian Economics Association, Vol. 21, Pgs. 187-99, February.

Trade, Global Policy, and the Environment, Pg. 56, Fredriksson, World Bank, World Bank Publications, 1999.

10

Environmental Audits

Environmental audit is a general term that can reflect various types or evaluations intended to quantify environmental performance/compliance. In this way they perform an analogous (similar) function to financial audits. There are generally two different types of environmental audits: compliance audits and management systems audits. Compliance audits tend to be the primary type in the US or within US-based multinationals.

Environmental Compliance Audits

As the name implies, these audits are intended to review the site's/company's legal compliance status. Compliance audits generally begin with determining the applicable compliance requirements against which the operations will be assessed. This tends to include federal regulations, state regulations, permits and local ordinances/codes. In some cases, it may also include requirements within legal settlements.

Compliance audits may be *multimedia* or *programmatic*. Multimedia audits involve identifying and auditing all environmental media (air, water, waste, etc.) that apply to the operation/company. Programmatic audits (which may also be called *thematic* or *media-specific*) are limited in scope to pre-identified regulatory areas, such as air.

Audits are also focused on operational aspects of a company/site, rather than the contamination status of the real property.

ISO 14001

ISO 14001 is a voluntary international standard for environmental management systems ("EMS"). ISO 14001:2004 provides the requirements for an EMS and ISO 14004:2004 gives general EMS guidelines. An EMS meeting the requirements of ISO 14001:2004 is a management tool enabling an organization of any size or type to: (1) identify and control the environmental impact of its activities, products or services; (2) improve its environmental performance continually, and (3) implement a systematic approach to setting environmental objectives and targets, to achieving these and to demonstrating that they have been achieved.

The goal of ISO 14001 implementation is to obtain certification. This indicates that the environmental procedures, systems and documentation standards conform to the established ISO14001 standard. A common misconception is that ISO certification directly reflects legal compliance. Certification under ISO 14001 does not directly reflect compliance with any legal requirements.

Audit Processes, Methods and Tools

The term "protocol" means the checklist used by environmental auditors as the guide for conducting the audit activities. Current technology supports many versions of computer-based protocols that attempt to simplify the audit process by converting regulatory requirements into questions with "yes", "no" and "not applicable" check boxes. Many companies and auditors find these useful and there are several such protocol systems commercially available.

Other auditors (typically those with many years of environmental auditing experience) use the regulations/permits directly as protocols.

In the US, permits for air emissions, wastewater discharges and other operational aspects, many times establish the primary legal compliance standards for companies. In these cases, auditing only to the regulations is inadequate. However, as these permits are site specific, standard protocols are not commercially available that reflect every permit condition for every company/site. Therefore, permit holders and the auditors they hire must identify the permit requirements and determine the most effective way to audit against those requirements.

During the past 20 years, advances in technology have had major impacts on auditing. Laptop computers, portable printers, CD/DVDs, the internet, email and wireless internet access have all been used to improve audits, increase/improve auditor access to regulatory information and create audit reports on-site. At one point in the 1990's, one major company invested significant resources in testing "video audits" where the auditor (located at the corporate headquarters) used real-time video conferencing technology to direct staff at a site to carry live video cameras to specific areas of the plant. While initially promising, this technology/concept did not prove acceptable.

The current "disruptive technology" in environmental auditing is Apple Computer's iPad. At this time, one audit consulting firm is using the iPad extensively for environmental audits, which includes specific protocols for the new technology.

Related Types of Assessments

Phase I Environmental Site Assessments ("ESA") are generally done in relation to mergers, acquisitions or financing activities. The intent of ESAs is to identify potential sources/existence of property contamination for purposes of clean up costs/liability under US law. ESA's rarely contain a compliance audit component and should not be confused with audits.

11

Conclusion

Environmental economics is a subfield of economics concerned with environmental issues. Quoting from the National Bureau of Economic Research Environmental Economics program:

> "[...] Environmental Economics [...] undertakes theoretical or empirical studies of the economic effects of national or local environmental policies around the world [...]. Particular issues include the costs and benefits of alternative environmental policies to deal with air pollution, water quality, toxic substances, solid waste, and global warming."

Central to environmental economics is the concept of market failure. Market failure means that markets fail to allocate resources efficiently. As stated by Hanley, Shogren, and White (2007) in their textbook *Environmental Economics*: "A market failure occurs when the market does not allocate scarce resources to generate the greatest social welfare. A wedge exists between what a private person does given market prices and what society might want him or her to do to protect the environment. Such a wedge implies wastefulness or economic inefficiency; resources can be reallocated to make at least one person better off without making anyone else worse off." Common forms of market failure include externalities, non-excludability and non-rivalry.

Externality: the basic idea is that an externality exists when a person makes a choice that affects other people that are not accounted for in the market price. For instance, a firm emitting pollution will typically not take into account the costs that its pollution imposes on others. As a result, pollution in excess of the 'socially efficient' level may occur. A classic definition influenced by Kenneth Arrow and James Meade is provided by Heller and Starrett (1976), who define an externality as "a situation in which the private economy lacks sufficient incentives to create a potential market in some good and the nonexistence of this market results in losses of Pareto efficiency."

In economic terminology, externalities are examples of market failures, in which the unfettered market does not lead to an efficient outcome. Common property and non-exclusion: When it is too costly to exclude people from access to an environmental resource for which there is rivalry, market allocation is likely to be inefficient. The challenges related with common property and non-exclusion have long been recognized. Hardin's (1968) concept of the tragedy of the commons popularized the challenges involved in non-exclusion and common property. "commons" refers to the environmental asset itself, "common property resource" or "common pool resource" refers to a property right regime that allows for some collective body to devise schemes to exclude others, thereby allowing the capture of future benefit streams; and "open-access" implies no ownership in the sense that property everyone owns nobody owns.

The basic problem is that if people ignore the scarcity value of the commons, they can end up expending too much effort, over harvesting a resource (e.g., a fishery). Hardin theorizes that in the absence of restrictions, users of an open-access resource will use it more than if they had to pay for it and had exclusive rights, leading to environmental degradation. See, however, Ostrom's (1990) work on how people using real common property resources have worked to establish self-governing rules to reduce the risk of the tragedy of the commons.

Public goods and non-rivalry: Public goods are another type of market failure, in which the market price does not capture the social benefits of its provision. For example, protection from the risks of climate change is a public good since its provision is both non-rival and non-excludable. Non-rival means climate protection provided to one country does not reduce the level of protection to another country; non-excludable means it is too costly to exclude any one from receiving climate protection. A country's incentive to invest in carbon abatement is reduced because it can "free ride" off the efforts of other countries.

Over a century ago, Swedish economist Knut Wicksell (1896) first discussed how public goods can be under-provided by the market because people might conceal their preferences for the good, but still enjoy the benefits without paying for them.

Assessing the economic value of the environment is a major topic within the field. Use and indirect use are tangible benefits accruing from natural resources or ecosystem services. Non-use values include existence, option, and bequest values. For example, some people may value the existence of a diverse set of species, regardless of the effect of the loss of a species cn ecosystem services. The existence of these species may have an option value, as there may be possibility of using it for some human purpose (certain plants may be researched for drugs). Individuals may value the ability to leave a pristine environment to their children.

Use and indirect use values can often be inferred from

revealed behavior, such as the cost of taking recreational trips or using hedonic methods in which values are estimated based on observed prices. Non-use values are usually estimated using stated preference methods such as contingent valuation or choice modelling. Contingent valuation typically takes the form of surveys in which people are asked how much they would pay to observe and recreate in the environment (willingness to pay) or their willingness to accept (WTA) compensation for the destruction of the environmental good. Hedonic pricing examines the effect the environment has on economic decisions through housing prices, traveling expenses, and payments to visit parks.

Solutions advocated to correct such externalities include:

- *Environmental regulations.* Under this plan, the economic impact has to be estimated by the regulator. Usually this is done using cost-benefit analysis. There is a growing realization that regulations (also known as "command and control" instruments) are not so distinct from economic instruments as is commonly asserted by proponents of environmental economics. E.g.1 regulations are enforced by fines, which operate as a form of tax if pollution rises above the threshold prescribed. E.g.2 pollution must be monitored and laws enforced, whether under a pollution tax regime or a regulatory regime. The main difference an environmental economist would argue exists between the two methods, however, is the total cost of the regulation. "Command and control" regulation often applies uniform emissions limits on polluters, even though each firm has different costs for emissions reductions. Some firms, in this system, can abate inexpensively, while others can only abate at high cost. Because of this, the total abatement has some expensive and some inexpensive efforts to abate. Environmental economic regulations find the cheapest emission abatement efforts first, then the more expensive methods second. E.g. as said earlier, trading, in the quota system, means a firm only abates if doing so would cost less than paying someone else to make the same reduction. This leads to a lower cost for the total abatement effort as a whole.

- *Quotas on pollution.* Often it is advocated that pollution reductions should be achieved by way of tradeable emissions permits, which if freely traded may ensure that reductions in pollution are achieved at least cost. In theory, if such tradeable quotas are allowed, then a firm would reduce its own pollution load only if doing so would cost less than paying someone else to make the same reduction. In practice, tradeable permits approaches have had some success, such as the U.S.'s sulphur dioxide trading program or the EU Emissions Trading Scheme, and interest in its application is spreading to other environmental problems.
- *Taxes and tariffs on pollution/Removal of "dirty subsidies."* Increasing the costs of polluting will discourage polluting, and will provide a "dynamic incentive," that is, the disincentive continues to operate even as pollution levels fall. A pollution tax that reduces pollution to the socially "optimal" level would be set at such a level that pollution occurs only if the benefits to society (for example, in form of greater production) exceeds the costs. Some advocate a major shift from taxation from income and sales taxes to tax on pollution - the so-called "green tax shift."

- *Better defined property rights*. The Coase Theorem states that assigning property rights will lead to an optimal solution, regardless of who receives them, if transaction costs are trivial and the number of parties negotiating is limited. For example, if people living near a factory had a right to clean air and water, or the factory had the right to pollute, then either the factory could pay those affected by the pollution or the people could pay the factory not to pollute. Or, citizens could take action themselves as they would if other property rights were violated. The US River Keepers Law of the 1880s was an early example, giving citizens downstream the right to end pollution upstream themselves if government itself did not act (an early example of bioregional democracy). Many markets for "pollution rights" have been created in the late twentieth century—see emissions trading. The assertion that defining property rights is a solution is controversial within the field of environmental economics and environmental law and policy more broadly; in Anglo-American and many other legal systems, one has the right to carry out any action unless the law expressly proscribes it. Thus, property rights are already assigned (the factory that is polluting has a right to pollute).

Environmental economics is related to ecological economics but there are differences. Most environmental economists have been trained as economists. They apply the tools of economics to address environmental problems, many of which are related to so-called market failures—circumstances wherein the "invisible hand" of economics is unreliable. Most ecological economists have been trained as ecologists, but have expanded the scope of their work to consider the impacts of humans and their economic activity on ecological systems and services, and vice-versa. This field takes as its premise that economics is a strict subfield of ecology. Ecological economics is sometimes described as taking a more pluralistic approach to environmental problems and focuses more explicitly on long-term environmental sustainability and issues of scale.

Environmental economics is viewed as more pragmatic in a price system; ecological economics as more idealistic in its attempts not use money as a primary arbiter of decisions. These two groups of specialists sometimes have conflicting views which may be traced to the different philosophical underpinnings.

Another context in which externalities apply is when globalization permits one player in a market who is unconcerned with biodiversity to undercut prices of another who is - creating a "race to the bottom" in regulations and conservation. This in turn may cause loss of natural capital with consequent erosion, water purity problems, diseases, desertification, and other outcomes which are not efficient in an economic sense. This concern is related to the subfield of sustainable development and its political relation, the anti-globalization movement.

Environmental economics was once distinct from resource economics. Natural resource economics as a subfield began when the main concern of researchers was the optimal commercial exploitation of natural resource stocks. But resource managers and policy-makers eventually began to pay attention to the broader importance of natural resources (e.g. values of fish and trees beyond just their commercial exploitation;, externalities associated with mining). It is now difficult to distinguish "environmental" and "natural resource" economics as separate fields as the two became associated with sustainability. Many of the more radical green economists split off to work on an alternate political economy.

Environmental economics was a major influence for the theories of natural capitalism and environmental finance, which could be said to be two sub-branches of environmental economics concerned with resource conservation in production, and the value of biodiversity to humans, respectively. The theory of natural capitalism (Hawken, Lovins, Lovins) goes further than traditional environmental economics by envisioning a world where natural services are considered on par with physical capital.

The more radical Green economists reject neoclassical economics in favour of a new political economy beyond capitalism or communism that gives a greater emphasis to the interaction of the human economy and the natural environment, acknowledging that "economy is three-fifths of ecology" - Mike Nickerson.

These more radical approaches would imply changes to money supply and likely also a bioregional democracy so that political, economic, and ecological "environmental limits" were all aligned, and not subject to the arbitrage normally possible under capitalism.

The main academic and professional organizations for the discipline of Environmental Economics are the Association of Environmental and Resource Economists (AERE) and the European Association for Environmental and Resource Economics (EAERE). The main academic and professional organization for the discipline of Ecological Economics is the International Society for Ecological Economics (ISEE) and The Green Economics Institute for Green Economics [greeneconomics.org.uk] is its international Professional body.

Environmental Finance

Environmental finance is the use of various financial instruments (most notably land trusts) to protect biodiversity. The field is part of both environmental economics and the conservation movement.

Dr. Gretchen Daily, of Stanford University has written a book, *The New Economy of Nature* that addresses the issue of financing ecosystem services.

Dr. Jürg P. Blum, defined the term environmental finance (Dissertation: Corporate Environmental Responsibility and Corporate Economic Performance..... 1994 at USIU)as a fairly new field, "concerned mainly with finance and investment regarding the ecological environment. The term environment, although frequently used in areas, such as strategic management (Ansoff, 1968), has been popularized throughout literature synonymously with the term ecological environment."

REFERENCES

Allen K. Kneese and Clifford S. Russell (1987). "environmental economics," *The New Palgrave: A Dictionary of Economics*, v. 2, pp. 159–64.

David Pearce (2002). "An Intellectual History Of Environmental Economics", Annual Review of Energy and the Environment 2002, 27:57–81.

Maureen L. Cropper and Wallace E. Oates (1992). "Environmental Economics: A Survey," *Journal of Economic Literature*, 30(2), pp. 675-740(press +).

Robert N. Stavins (2008). "environmental economics," *The New Palgrave Dictionary of Economics*, 2nd Edition. Abstract & article.

UNEP (2007). Guidelines for Conducting Economic Valuation of Coastal Ecosystem Goods and Services, UNEP/GEF/SCS Technical Publication No. 8.

UNEP (2007). Procedure for Determination of National and Regional Economic Values for Ecotone Goods and Services, and Total Economic Values of Coastal Habitats in the context of the UNEP/GEF Project Entitled: "Reversing Environmental Degradation Trends in the South China Sea and Gulf of Thailand", South China Sea Knowledge Document No. 3. UNEP/GEF/SCS/Inf.3

Appendix

The United Nations Conference on the Human Environment*

Having met at Stockholm from 5 to June 1972

Having considered the need for a common outlook and for common principles to inspire and guide the peoples of the world in the preservational and enhancement of the human environment.

I

PROCLAIMS THAT

1. Man is both creature and moulder of his environment, which gives him physical sustenance and affords him the opportunity for intellectual, moral, social and spiritual growth. In the long and tortuous evolution of the human race on this planet a stage has been reached when, through the rapid acceleration of science and technology, man has acquired the power to transform his environment in countless ways on an unprecedented scale. Both aspects of man's environment, the natural and the man-made, are essential to his well-being and to the enjoyment of basic human rights even the right to life itself.
2. The protection and improvement of the human environment is a major issue which effect the well-being of peoples and economic development throughout the world; it is the urgent desire of the

people of the whole world and the duty of all Governments.

3. Man has constantly to sum up experience can go on discovering, inventing, creating and advancing. In our time, man's capacity to transform his surroundings, if used wisely, can bring to all peoples the benefits of development and the opportunity to enhance the equality of the life. Wrongly or needlessly applied, the same power can do incalculable harm to human beings and the human environment. We see around us growing evidence of man-made harm in many regions of the earth; dangerous levels of pollution in water, air, earth and living beings; major and undesirable disturbances to the ecological balance of the biosphere destruction and depletion of irreplaceable resources; and gross deficiencies harmful to the physical, mental and social health of man, is the man-made environment, particularly in the living and working environment.

4. In the developing countries most of the environmental problems are caused by under development. Millions continue too live far below the minimum levels required for a decent human existence, deprived of adequate food and clothing, shelter and education, health and sanitation. Therefore, the developing countries must direct their efforts to development, bearing in mind their priorities and the need to safeguard and improve the environment. For the same purpose, the industrialized countries should make efforts to reduce the gap between themselves and the developing countries. In the industrialized countries, environmental problems are generally related to industrialization and technological development.

5. The natural growth of population continuously presents problems on the preservation of the environment, and adequate policies and measures should be adopted, as appropriate, to face these problems. Of all things in the world, people are the most precious. It is the people that propel social progress, create social wealth, develop science and technology and, through their hard work, continuously transform the human environment. Along with social progress and the advance of production, science and technology, the capability of man to improve the environment increases with each passing

6. A point has been reached in history when we must shape our actions throughout the world with a more predent care for their environmental consequences. Through ignorance or indifference we can do massive and irreversible harm to the earthly environment on which our life and well-being depend Conversely, through fuller knowledge and wise action, we can achieve of ourselves and our posterity a better life in an environment more in keeping with human needs and hopes. There are broad vistas for the enhancement of environmental quality and the creation of a good life. What is needed is an enthusiastic but calm state of mind and intense but orderly work. For the purpose of attaining freedom in the world of nature, man must use knowledge to build, in collaboration with nature, a better environment. To defend and improve the human environment for present and future generations has become an imperative goal for mankind—a goal to be pursued together with, and in harmony with, the established

and fundamental goals of peace and of world-wide economic and social development.

7. To achieve this environmental goal will demand the acceptance of responsibility by citizens and communities and by enterprises and institutions at every level, all sharing equitably in common efforts. Individuals in all walk of life as well as organisations in many fields, by their values and the sum of their actions, will shape the world environment of the future. Local and national governments will bear the greatest burden for large-scale environmental policy and action within their jurisdictions. International co-operations also needed in order to raise resource to support the developing countries in carrying out their responsibilities in this field A growing class of environmental problem, because they are regional or global in extent or because they affect the common international realm, will require extensive co-operation among nations and action by international organizations in the common interest. The Conference calls upon Governments and peoples to exert common efforts for the preservation and improvement of the human environment, for the benefit of all the people and for their posterity.

II
PRINCIPLES

State the Common Conviction That

Principle 1

Man has the fundamental right to freedom, equality and adequate conditions of life. In an environment of a quality that permits life of dignity and well-being, the bears a solemn responsibility to project and improve the environment for present and future generations. In this respect, policies promoting or perpetuating apartheid, racial segregation, discrimination, colonial and other forms of oppression and foreign domination stand condemned and must be eliminated.

Principle 2

The natural resources of the earth including the air, water, land, flora and fauna and especially representative samples of natural eco-system must be safeguard for the benefit of present and future generations through careful planning or management, as appropriate.

Principle 3

The capacity of the earth to produce vital renewable resources must be maintained and, wherever practicable, restored or improved.

Principle 4

Man has a special responsibility to safeguard and wisely manage the heritage of wildlife and its habitats which are now gravely imperilled by a combination of adverse factors. Nature conservation including wildlife must therefore receive importance in planning for economic development.

Principle 5

The non-renewable resources of the earth must be employed in such a way as to guard against the danger of their future exhausting and to ensure that benefits from such employment are shared by all mankind.

Principle 6

The discharge to toxic substance or of other substances and the release of heat, in such quantities or concentrations as to exceed the capacity of the environment to render them harmless, must be halted in order to ensure that serious or irreversible damage is not inflicted upon ecosystems. The just struggle of the peoples of all countries against pollution should be supported.

Principle 7

States shall take all possible steps to prevent pollution of the seas by substances that are liable to create hazard to human health to harm living resources and marine life, to damage amenities or to interfere with other legitimate uses of the sea.

Principle 8

Economic and social development is essential for ensuring favourable living and working environment for man and for creating conditions on earth that are necessary for the improvement of the quality of life.

Principle 9

Environment deficiencies generated by the conditions of underdevelopment and natural disasters poses grave problems and can best be remedied by accelerated development through the transfer of substantial quantities of financial and technological assistance as a supplement to the domestic effort of the developing countries and such timely assistance as may be required.

Principle 10

For the developing countries, stability of prices and adequate earnings for primary commodities and raw material are essential to environmental management since economic factors as well as ecological processes must be taken into account.

Principle 11

The environment policies of all States should enhance and not adversely affect the present or future of developing countries, nor should they hamper the attainment of better living conditions for all, and appropriate steps should be taken by states and international organizations with a view to reaching agreement on meeting the possible national and international economic consequences resulting from the application of environmental measures.

Principle 12

Resources should be made available to preserve and improve the environment, taking into account the circumstances and particular requirements of developing countries and any costs which may emenate from their incorporating environmental safeguards into their development planning and the need for making available to them, upon their request, additional international technical and financial assistance for this purpose.

Principle 13

In order to achieve a more rational management of resources and thus to improve the environment, states should adopt an integrated and co-ordinated approach to their development planning so as to ensure that development is compatible with the need to protect and improve the human environment for the benefit of their population.

Principle 14

Rational planning constitutes an essential too for reconciling any conflict between the needs of development and the need to protect and improve the environments.

Principle 15

Planning must be applied to human settlements and urbanization with a view of avoiding adverse in this respect projects which are designed for colonialist and racist domination must be abandoned.

Principle 16

Demographic policies, which are without prejudice to basis human rights and which are deemed appropriate by Governments concerned, should be applied in those regions where the rate of population growth or excessive population concentrations are likely to have adverse effects on the environment or development, or where low population density may prevent improvement of the human environment and impede development.

Principle 17

Appropriate national institutions must be entrusted with the task of planning managing or controlling the environmental quality.

Principle 18

Science and technology, as part of their contribution to economic and social development, must be applied to the identification, avoidance and control of environmental risks and the solution of environmental problems and for the common good mankind.

Principle 19

Education in environment matter, for the younger generation as well as adults, giving due consideration to the underprivileged, is essential in order to broaden the basis for all enlightened opinion and responsible conduct by individuals, enterprises and communities in protection and improving environment in its full human dimension. It is also essential that mass media of communications avoid contributing to the deterioration of the environment, but, on the contrary, disseminate information of an educational nature, on the need to protect and improve the environment in order to enable man to develop in every respect.

Principle 20

Scientific research and development in the context of environment problems, both national and multinational, must be promoted all countries, especially the developing countries. In this connection, the free flow of up-to date scientific information and transfer of experience must be supported and assisted, to facilitate the solution of environmental problems; environmental technologies should be made available to developing countries on terms which would encourage their wide dissemination without constituting an economic burden on the developing countries.

Principle 21

State have, in accordance with the Charter of the United Nations and the principles of International law, the sovereign right to exploit their own resources pursuant to their own environmental policy, and the responsibility to ensure that activities within their jurisdiction or control do not cause damage to the environment of other state or of areas beyond the limits of national jurisdiction.

Principle 22

States shall co-operate to develop further the international law regarding liability and compensation for the victims of pollution and other environmental damage caused by activities within the jurisdiction or control of such States or areas beyond their jurisdiction.

Principle 23

Without prejudice to such criteria as may be agreed upon by the international community; or to standards which will have to be determined nationally, it will be essential in all cases to consider the systems of values prevailing in each country, and the extent of the applicability of standards which are valid for the most advanced countries but which may be inappropriate and of unwarranted social cost for the developing countries.

Principle 24

International matters concerning the protection and improvement of the environment should be handled in a cooperative spirit by all countries, big or small, on an equal footing. Co-operations through multilateral or bilateral arrangements or other appropriate means is essential to effectively control. Prevent, reduce and eliminate adverse environmental effects resulting from activities conducted in all spheres, in such a way that due account is taken of the sovereignty and interests of all States.

Principle 25

States shall ensure that international organizations play a coordinated, efficient and dynamic role for the protection and improvement of the environment.

Principle 26

Man and his environment must be spared of the effects nuclear weapons and all other means of mass destruction. States must strive to teach prompt agreement, in the relevant international organs, on the elimination and complete destruction of such weapons.

An assessment after ten years of the Stockholm Conference, suggested that man's perception of the natural world had changed. Notable advances had taken place in the scientific means of examining the complex and interrelated systems of the biosphere, and space research had provided means for large scale monitoring of the earth, its resources and its processes.

Increased emphasis had been placed during the decade on environmental education and public awareness with nongovernmental organisation playing an important role, consequently, environmental issues have come to be better perceived. It is not appreciated that all environmental systems are closely inter-connected, and are subject to natural and man-made changes which in some cases are irreversible.

There has been a massive expansion in the establishment of national environmental bodies and in legislation dealing with environmental issue. Good amount of work has been done also through the United Nations system. With the establishment of the United Nations Environment Programme (UNEP) in 1982 and UN Centre for Human Settlement (UNCHS) later, the environmental activities have been receiving a sharper focus. Various specialised agencies on the UN system such UNDP, UNIDO, FAO, WHO and WMO (World Meteorological Organisation) have also given added emphasis in their programme on issues of environmental concern.

However, the overall state of the natural environment has not improved; indeed, deterioration is proceeding at accelerated rates in a number of its components.

UNEP SESSION OF SPECIAL CHARACTER

In May 1982, UNEP convened in Nairobi a Session of a Special Character (SSC) of the Governing Council of UNEP to commemorate the tenth anniversary of the Stockholm Conference of the Human Environment. The Session reviewed major achievements of the Stockholm Action Plan and recommended action in the field of the environment to be taken by UNEP over the next 10 years.

The Conference adopted a "Nairobi Declaration" and decision "Environment in 1982—Retrospect and prospect". The Conference felt that the principles of declaration of the Stockholm Conference were as valid today as they were in 1982 and together with the decisions adopted in the Nairobi Conference provided basic guidelines for effective and sustained environmental progress.

The Conference identified the basic orientation of the United Nations Environment Programme for 1982-1992. It charged UNEP to focus its attention on assessment of environmental problems of world wide concern; promotion of appropriate programmes for resource and environmental managemental management as an integral part of development with particular attention to the needs of developing countries, and promotion of environmental law and guidelines.

The Conference suggested that in pursuing these objectives UNEP should be guided by major environmental trends, potential problems and priorities of action (Kindly refer Annexure) and should concentrate in particular on:

- (i) Promotion of land and water management, including control of desertification and deforestation;
- (ii) Promotion of natural resources;
- (iii) Promotion of the International Drinking Water and Sanitation Decade;
- (iv) Promotion of new and renewable sources of energy;
- (v) Promotion of regional seas programmes;
- (vi) Prevention of environmental disturbances from air pollution;
- (vii) Prevention of chemical safety and control of hazardous substances.

The Conference asked all governments, inter-governments organisations and non-governmental organisations to ensure that the priorities for action was accorded high priority within respectic programme.

AIR POLLUTION ACT, 1981*

An Act to provide for the prevention control and abatement of air pollution, for the establishment, with a view to carrying out the aforesaid purposes, of Boards powers and functions relating thereto and for matters connected therewith.

Whereas decisions were taken at the United Nations Conference on the Human Environment held in Stockholm in June, 1972, in which India participated, to take appropriate steps for the preservation of the natural resources of the earth which, among other things, include the preservation of the quality of air and control of air pollution;

And Whereas it is considered necessary to implement the decisions aforesaid in so far as they relate to the preservation of the quality of air and control of air pollution;

Be it enacted by Parliament in the Thirty-second Year of the Republic of India as follows:-

CHAPTER I

Preliminary

Short Title, Extent and Commencement

1. (1) This Act may be called the Air (Prevention and Control of Pollution) Act, 1981.

   (2) It extends to the whole of India.

   (3) It shall come into force on such date as the Central Government may, by notification in the Official Gazette, appoint.

Definitions

2. In this Act, unless the context otherwise requires,-

(a) "air pollutant" means any solid, liquid or gaseous substance (including noise) present in the atmosphere in such concentration as may be or tend to be injurious to human beings or other living creatures or plants or property or environment;

(b) "air pollution" means the presence, in the atmosphere of any air pollutant;

(c) "approved appliances" means any equipment or gadget used for the bringing of any combustible material or for generating or consuming any fume, gas of particulate matter and approved by the State Board for the purpose of this Act;

(d) "approved fuel" means any fuel approved by the State Board for the purposes of this Act;

(e) "automobile" means any vehicle powered either by internal combustion engine or by any method of generating power to drive such vehicle by burning fuel;

(f) "Board" means the Central Board or State Board;

(g) "Central Board" means the (Central Board for the Prevention and Control of Water Pollution) constituted under section 3 of the Water (Prevention and Control of Pollution) Act, 1974;

(h) "chimney" includes any structure with an opening or outlet from or through which any air pollutant may be emitted;

(i) "control equipment' means any apparatus, device, equipment or system to control the quality and manner of emission of any air pollutant and includes any device used for securing the efficient operation of any industrial plant;

(j) "emission" means any solid or liquid or gaseous substance coming out of any chimney, duct or flue or any other outlet;

(k) "industrial plant" means any plant used for any industrial or trade purposes and emitting any air pollutant into the atmosphere;

(l) "member" means a member of the Central Board or a State Board, as the case may be, and includes the Chairman thereof;

(m) "occupier," in relation to any factory or premises, means the person who has control over the affairs of the factory or the premises, and includes, in relation to any substance, the person in possession of the substance;

(n) "prescribed" means prescribed by rules made under this Act by the Central Government or as the case may be, the State Government-

(o) "State Board" means,-

(i) In relation to a State in which the Water (Prevention and Control of Pollution) Act, 1974, is in force and the State Government has constituted for that State a (State Board for the Prevention and Control of Water Pollution) under section 4 of that Act, the said State Board; and

(ii) in relation to any other State, the State Board for the Prevention and Control of Air Pollution constituted by the State Government under section 5 of this Act.

CHAPTER II

Central and State Boards for the Prevention and Control of Air Pollution

Central Board for the Prevention and Control of Air Pollution

3. The Central Board for the Prevention and Control of Water Pollution constituted under section 3 of the Water (Prevention and Control of Pollution) Act, 1974 (6 of 1974), shall, without prejudice to the exercise and performance of its powers and functions under this Act, exercise the powers and perform the functions of the Central Board for the Prevention and Control of Air Pollution under this Act.

State Boards for the Prevention and Control of Water Pollution to be State Boards for the Prevention and Control of Air Pollution

4. In any State in which the Water (Prevention and Control of Pollution) Act, 1974 (6 of 1974), is in force and the State Government has constituted for that State a State Board for the Prevention and Control of Water Pollution under section 4 of that Act, such State Board shall be deemed to be the State Board for the Prevention and Control of Air Pollution constituted under section 5 of this Act and accordingly that State Board for the Prevention and Control of Water Pollution shall, without prejudice to the exercise and performance of its powers and functions under that Act, exercise the powers and perform the functions of the State Board for the Prevention and Control of Air Pollution under this Act.

Constitution of State Boards

5.(1) In any State in. which the Water (Prevention and Control of Pollution) Act, 1974 (6 of 1974), is not in force, or that Act is in force but the State Government has not constituted a (State Board for the Prevention and Control of Water Pollution) under that Act, the State Government shall, with effect from such date as it may, by notification in the Official Gazette, appoint, constitute a State Board for the Prevention and Control of Air Pollution under such name as may be specified in the notification, to exercise the powers conferred on, and perform the functions assigned to, that Board under this Act.

(2) A State Board constituted under this Act shall consist of the following members, namely:-

(a) a Chairman, being a person, having a person having special knowledge or practical experience in respect of matters relating to environmental protection, to be nominated by the State Government:

Provided that the Chairman may be either whole-time or part-time as the State Government may think fit;

(b) Such number of officials, not exceeding five, as the State Government may think fit, to be nominated by the State Government to represent that government;

(c) such number of persons, not exceeding five, as the State Government may think fit, to be nominated by the State Government from amongst the members of the local authorities functioning within the State;

(d) such number of non-officials, not exceeding three, as the State Government may think fit, to be nominated by the State Government to represent the interest of agriculture, fishery or industry or trade or labour or any other interest, which in the opinion of that government, ought to be represented;

(e) two persons to represent the companies or corporations owned, controlled or managed by the State Government, to be nominated by that Government;

(f) a full-time member-secretary having such qualifications knowledge and experience of scientific, engineering or management aspects of pollution control as may be prescribed, to be appointed by the State Government.

Provided that the State Government shall ensure that not less than two of the members are persons having special knowledge or practical experience in respect of matters relating to the improvement of the quality of air or the prevention, control or abatement of air pollution.

(3) Every State Board constituted under this Act shall be a body corporate with the name specified by the State Government in the notification issued under sub-section (1), having perpetual succession and a common seal with power, subject to the provisions of this Act, to acquire and dispose of property and to contract, and may be the said name sue or be sued.

Central Board to Exercise the Powers and Perform the Functions of a State Board in the Union territories

6. No State Board shall be constituted for a Union territory and in relation to a Union territory, the Central Board shall exercise the powers and perform the functions of a State Board under this Act for that Union territory:

Provided that in relation to any Union territory the Central Board may delegate all or any of its powers and functions under this section to such person or body of persons as the Central Government may specify.

Terms and Conditions of Service of Members

7. (1) Save as otherwise provided by or under this Act, a member of a State Board constituted under this Act, other than the member-secretary, shall hold office for a term of three years from the date on which his nomination is notified in the Official Gazette:

Provided that a member shall, notwithstanding the expiration of his term, continue to hold office until his successor enters upon his office.

(2) The terms of office of a member of a State Board constituted under this Act and nominated under clause (b) or clause (e) of sub-section (2) of section 5 shall come to an end as soon as he ceases to hold the office under the State Government as the case may be, the company or corporation owned, controlled or managed by the State Government, by virtue of which he was nominated.

(3) A member of a State Board constituted under this Act, other than the member-secretary, may at any time resign his office by writing under his hand addressed,-

(a) in the case of the Chairman, to the State Government; and

(b) in any other case, to the Chairman of the State Board, and the seat of the Chairman or such other member shall thereupon become vacant.

(4) A member of a State Board constituted under this Act, other than the member-secretary, shall be deemed to have vacated his seat, if he is absent without reason, sufficient in the opinion of the State Board, from three consecutive meetings of the State Board or where he is nominated under clause (c) of sub-section (2) of section 5, he ceases to be a member of the local authority and such vacation of seat shall, in either case, take effect from such as the State Government *may, by* notification in the Official Gazette, specify.

(5) A casual vacancy in a State Board constituted under this Act shall be filled by a fresh nomination and the person nominated to fill the vacancy shall hold office only for the remainder of the term for which the member whose place he takes was nominated.

(6) A member of a State Board constituted under this Act shall be eligible for re-nomination

(7) The other terms and conditions of service of the Chairman and other members (except the member-secretary) of a State Board constituted under this Act shall be such as may be prescribed.

Disqualifications

8. (1) No person shall be a member of a State Board constituted under this Act, who-

(a) is, or at any time has been, adjudged insolvent, or

(b) is of unsound mind and has been so declared by a competent court, or

(c) is, or has been, convicted of an offence which, in the opinion of the State Government, involves moral turpitude, or

(d) is, or at any time has been, convicted of an offence under this Act, or

(e) has directly or indirectly by himself on by any partner, any share or interest in any firm or company carrying on the business of manufacture, sale, or hire of machinery, industrial plant, control equipment or any other apparatus for the improvement of the quality of air or for the prevention', control or abatement of air pollution, or

(f) is a director or a secretary, manager or other salaried officer or employee of any company or firm having any contract with the Board, or with the Government constituting the Board or with a local authority in the State, or with a company or corporation owned, controlled or managed by the Government, for the carrying out of programmes for the improvement of the quality of air or for the prevention, control or abatement of air pollution, or

(g) has so abused, in the opinion of the State Government, his position as a member, as to render his continuance on the State Board detrimental to the interest of the general public.

(2) The State Government shall, by order in writing, remove any member who is, or has become, subject to any disqualification mentioned in sub-section (1).

Provided that no order of removal shall be made by the State Government under this section unless the member concerned has been given a reasonable opportunity of showing cause against the same.

(3) Notwithstanding anything contained in sub-section (1) or sub-section (6) of section 7, a member who has been removed under this section shall not be eligible to continue to hold office until his successor enters upon his office, or, as the case may be, for re-nomination as a member.

Vacation of Seats by Members

9. If a member of a State Board constituted under this Act becomes subject to any of the disqualifications specified in section 8, his seat shall become vacant.

Meeting of Board

10. (1) For the purposes of this Act, a Board shall meet at least once in every three months and shall observe such rules of procedure in regard to the transaction of business at its meetings as may be prescribed:

Provided that if, in the opinion of the Chairman, any business of an urgent nature is to be transacted, he may convene a meeting of the Board at such time as he thinks fit for the aforesaid purpose.

(2) Copies of minutes of the meetings under sub-section (1) shall be forwarded to the State Board and to the State Government concerned.

Constitution of Committees

11. (1) A Board may constitute as many committees consisting wholly of members or partly of members and partly of other persons and for such purpose or purposes as it may think fit.

(2) A committee constituted under this section shall meet at such time and at such place, and shall observe such rules of procedure in regard to the transaction of business at its meetings, as may be prescribed.

(3) The members of a committee other than the members of the Board shall be paid such fees and allowances, for attending its meetings and for attending to any other work of the Board as may be prescribed.

Temporary Association of Persons with Board for Particular Purposes

12. (1) A Board may associate with itself in such manner, and for such purposes, as may be prescribed, any person whose assistance or advice it may desire to obtain in performing any of its functions under this Act.

(2) A person associated with the Board under sub-section (1) for any purpose shall have a right to take part in the discussions of the Board relevant to that purpose, but shall not have a right to vote at a meetings of the Board and shall not be a member of the Board for any other purpose.

(3) A person associated with a Board under sub-section (1) shall be entitled to receive such fees and allowances as may be prescribed.

Vacancy in Board not to Invalidate Acts or Proceedings

13. No act or proceeding of a Board or any committee thereof shall be called in question on the ground merely of the existence of any vacancy in or any defect in the constitution of, the Board or such committee, as the case may be.

Member-Secretary and Officers and Other Employees of State Boards

14. (l) The terms and conditions of service of the member-secretary of a State Board constituted under this Act shall be such as may be prescribed.

(2) The member-secretary of a State Board, whether

constituted under this Act or not, shall exercise such powers and perform such duties as may be prescribed or as may, from time to time, be delegated to him by the State Board or its Chairman.

(3) Subject to such rules as may be made by the State Government in this behalf, a State Board, whether constituted under this Act or not, may appoint such officers and other employees as it considers necessary for the efficient performance of its functions under this Act.

(4) The method of appointment, the conditions of service and the scale of pay of the officers (other than the member-secretary) and other employees of a State Board appointed under sub-section(3) shall be such as may be determined by regulations made by the State Board under this Act.

(5) Subject to such conditions as may be prescribed, a State Board constituted under this Act may from time to time appoint any qualified person to be a consultant to the Board and pay him such salary and allowances or fees, as it thinks fit.

Delegation of Powers

15. A State Board may, by general or special order, delegate to the Chairman or the member-secretary or any other officer of the Board subject to such conditions and limitations, if any, as may be specified in the order, such of its powers and functions under this Act as it may deem necessary.

CHAPTER III

Powers and Functions of Boards

Functions of Central Board

16. (1) Subject to the provisions of this Act, and without

prejudice to the performance, of its functions under the Water (Prevention and Control of Pollution) Act, 1974 (6 of 1974), the main functions of the Central Board shall be to improve the quality of air and to prevent, control or ovate air pollution in the country.

(2) In particular and without prejudice to the generality of the foregoing functions, the Central Board may-

(a) advise the Central Government on any matter concerning the improvement of the quality of air and the prevention, control or abatement of air pollution;

(b) plan and cause to be executed a nation-wide programme for the prevention, control or abatement of air pollution;

(c) co-ordinate the activities of the State and resolve disputes among them;

(d) provide technical assistance and guidance to the State Boards, carry out and sponsor investigations and research relating to problems of air pollution and prevention, control or abatement of air pollution;

(d) perform such function of any State Board as may be specified in and order made under subsection (2) of section 18;

(e) plan and organise the training of persons engaged or to be engaged in programmes for the prevention, control or abatement of air pollution on such terms and conditions as the Central Board may specify;

(f) organise through mass media a comprehensive programme regarding the prevention, control or abatement of air pollution;

(g) Collect, compile and publish technical and statistical data relating to air pollution and the measures devised for its effective prevention, control or abatement and prepare manuals, codes or guides relating to prevention, control or abatement of air pollution;

(h) lay down standards for the quality of air;

(i) collect and disseminate information in respect of matters relating to air pollution;

(j) perform such other functions as may be prescribed.

(3) The Central Board may establish or recognise a laboratory or laboratories to enable the Central Board to perform its functions under this section efficiently.

(4) The Central Board may-

(a) delegate any of its functions under this Act generally or specially to any of the committees appointed by it;

(b) do such other things and perform such other acts as it may think necessary for the proper discharge of its functions and generally for the purpose of carrying into effect the purposes of this Act.

Functions of State Boards

17. (1) Subject to the provisions of this Act, and without prejudice to the performance of its functions., if any, under the Water (Prevention and Control of

Pollution) Act, 1974 (Act 6 of 1974), the functions of a State Board shall be-

(a) to plan a comprehensive programme for the prevention, control of abatement of air pollution and to secure the execution thereof;

(b) to advise the State Government on any matter concerning the prevention, control or abatement of air pollution;

(c) to collect and disseminate information relating to air pollution;

(d) to collaborate with the Central Board in organising the training of persons engaged or to be engaged in programmes relating to prevention, control or abatement of air pollution and to organise mass-education programme relating thereto;

(e) to inspect, at all reasonable times, any control equipment, industrial plant or manufacturing process and to give, by order, such directions tosuch persons as it may consider necessary to fake steps for the prevention, control or abatement of air pollution;

(f) to inspect air pollution control areas at such intervals as it may think necessary, assess the quality of air therein and take steps for the prevention, control or abatement of air pollution in such areas;

(g) to lay down, in consultation with the Central Board and having regard to the standards for the quality of air laid down by the Central Board, standards for emission of air pollutants into the atmosphere from industrial plants and automobiles or for the discharge of any air pollutant into the atmosphere from any other source whatsoever not being a ship or an aircraft:

Provided that different standards for emission may be laid down under this clause for different industrial plants having regard to the quantity and composition of emission of air pollutants into the atmosphere from such industrial plants;

(h) to advise the State Government with respect to the suitability of any premises or location for carrying on any industry which is likely to cause air pollution;

(i) to perform such other functions as may be prescribed or as may, from time to time, be entrusted to it by the Central Board or the State Government;

(j) to do such other things and to perform such other acts as it may think necessary for the proper discharge of its functions and generally for the purpose of carrying into effect the purposes of this Act.

(2) A State Board may establish or recognise a laboratory or laboratories to enable the State Board to perform its functions under this section efficiently.

Power to Give Directions

18.(1) In the performance of its functions under this Act-

(a) the Central Board shall be bound by such directions in writing as the Central Government may give to it; and

(b) every State Board shall be bound by such

directions in writing as the Central Board or the State Government may give to it;

Provided that where a direction given by the State Government is inconsistent with the direction given by the Central Board, the matter shall be referred to the Central Government for its decision.

(2) Where the Central Government is of the opinion that any State Board has defaulted in complying with any directions given by the Central Board under sub-section (1) and as a result of such default a grave emergency has arisen and it is necessary or expedient so to do in the public interest, it may, by order, direct the Central Board to perform any of the functions of the State Board in relation to such area, for such period and for such purposes, as may be specified in the order.

(3) Where the Central Board performs any of the functions of the State Board in pursuance of a direction under sub-section (2), the expenses, if any incurred by the Central Board with respect to the performance of such functions may, if the State Board is empowered to recover such expenses, be recovered by the Central Board with interest (at such reasonable rate as the Central Government may, by order, fix) from the date when a demand for such expenses is made until it is paid from the person or persons concerned as arrears of land revenue or of public demand.

(4) For the removal of doubts, it is hereby declared that any directions to perform the functions of any State Board given under sub-section (2) in respect of any area would not preclude the State Board from performing such functions in any other area

in the State or any of its other functions in that area.

CHAPTER IV

Prevention and Control of Air Pollution

Power to Declare air Pollution Control Areas

19. (l) The State Government may, after consultation with the State Board, by notification in the Official Gazette declare in such manner as may be prescribed, any area or areas within the State as air pollution control area or areas for the purposes of this Act.

(2) The State Government may, after consultation with the State Board, by notification in the Official Gazette,

(a) alter any air pollution control area whether by way of extension or reduction;

(b) declare a new air pollution control area in which may be merged one or more existing air pollution control areas or any part or parts thereof.

(3) If the State Government, after consultation with the State Board, is of opinion that the use of any fuel, other than an approved fuel, in any air pollution control area or part thereof, may cause or is likely to cause air pollution, it may by notification in the Official Gazette, prohibit the use of such fuel in such area or part thereof with effect from such date (being not less than three months from the date of publication of the notification) as may be specified in the notification.

(4) The State Government may, after consultation with the State Board, by notification in the Official

Gazette, direct that with effect from such date as may be specified therein, no appliance, other than an approved appliance, shall be used in the premises situated in an air pollution control area:

Provided that different dates may be specified for different parts of an air pollution control area or for the use of different appliances.

(5) If the State Government, after consultation with the State Board, is of opinion that the burning of any material (not being fuel) in any air pollution control area or part thereof may cause or is likely to cause air pollution, it may, by notification in the Official Gazette, prohibit the burning of such material in such area or part thereof.

Powers to Give Instructions for Ensuring Standards for Emission from Automobiles

20. With a view to ensuring that the standards for emission of air pollutants from automobiles laid down by the State Board under clause (g) of subsection (1) of section 17 are complied with the State Government shall, in consultation with, the State Board, give such instructions as may be deemed necessary to the concerned authority in charge of registration of motor vehicles under the Motor Vehicle? Act,, 1939 (Act 4 of 1939), and such authority shall, notwithstanding anything contained in that Act or the rules made thereunder be bound to comply with such instructions.

Restrictions on Use of Certain Industrial Plants

21. (1) Subject to the provisions of this section, no person shall, without the previous consent of the State Board, establish or operate any industrial plant in an air pollution control area:

47 of 1987

Provided that a person operating any industrial plant in any air pollution control area immediately before the commencement of section 9 of the Air (Prevention and Control of Pollution) Amendment Act, 1987, for which no consent was necessary prior to such commencement, may continue to do so for a period of three months from such commencement or, if he has made an application for such consent within the said period of three months, till the disposal of such application.

(2) An application for consent of the State Board under sub-section(l) shall be accompanied by such fees as may be prescribed and shall be made in the prescribed form and shall contain the particulars of the industrial plant and such other particulars as may be prescribed:

Provided that where any person, immediately before the declaration of any area as an air pollution control area, operates in such area any industrial plant, such person shall make the application under this sub-section within such period (being not less than three months from the date of such declaration) as may be prescribed and where such person makes such application, he shall be deemed to be operating such industrial plant with the consent of the State Board until the consent applied for has been refused.

(3) The State Board may make such inquiry as it may deem fit in respect of the application for consent referred to in sub-section (1) and in making any such inquiry, shall follow such procedure as may be prescribed.

(4) Within a period of four months after the receipt of the application for consent referred to in sub-section (1), the State Board shall, by order in writing, (and for reasons to be recorded in the order, grant the

consent applied for subject to such conditions and for such period as may be specified in the order, or refuse consent.)

Provided that it shall be open to the State Board to cancel such consent before the expiry of the period for which it is granted or refuse further consent after such expiry if the conditions subject to which such consent has been granted are not fulfilled:

Provided further that before cancelling a consent or refusing a further consent under the first provision, a reasonable opportunity of being heard shall be given to the person concerned.

(5) Every person to whom consent has been granted by the State Board under sub-section (4), shall comply with the following conditions, namely:-

(i) the control equipment of such specifications as the State Board may approve in this behalf shall be installed and operated in the premises where the industry is carried on or proposed to be carried on;

(ii) the existing control equipment, if any, shall be altered or replaced in accordance with the directions of the State Board;

(iii) the control equipment referred to in clause (i) or clause (ii) shall be kept at all times in good running condition;

(iv) chimney, wherever necessary, of such specifications as the State Board may approve in this behalf shall be erected or re-erected in such premises;

(v) such other conditions as the State Board, may specify in this behalf; and

(vi) the conditions referred to in clauses (i), (ii) and (iv) shall be complied with within such period as the State Board may specify in this behalf:

Provided that in the case of a person operating any industrial plant in an air pollution control area immediately before the date of declaration of such area as an air pollution control area, the period so specified shall not be less than six months:

Provided Further That-

(a) after the installation of any control equipment in accordance with the specifications under clause (i), or

(b) after the alteration or replacement of any control equipment in accordance with the directions of the State Board under clause (ii), or

(c) after the erection or re-erection of any chimney under clause (iv), no control equipment or chimney shall be altered or replaced or, as the case may be, erected or re-erected except with the previous approval of the State Board.

(6) If clue to any technological improvement or otherwise me State Board is of opinion that all or any of the conditions referred to in sub section (5) require or requires variation (including the change of any control equipment, either in whole or in part), the State Board shall, after giving the person to whom consent has been granted an opportunity of being heard, vary all or any of such conditions and thereupon such person shall be bound to comply with the conditions as so varied.

(7) Where a person to whom consent has been granted by the State Board under sub-section (4) transfers his interest in the industry to any other person, such consent shall be deemed to have been granted to such other person and he shall be bound to comply with all the conditions subject to which it was granted as if the consent was granted to him originally.

Persons Carrying on Industry, Etc., Not to Allow Emission of air Pollutants in Excess of the Standards laid Down by State Board

22. No person operating any industrial plant, in any air pollution control area shall discharge or cause or permit to be discharged the emission of any air pollutant in excess of the standards laid down by the State Board under clause (g) of sub-section (1) of section 17.

Power of Board to Make Application to Court for Restraining Persons from causing Air Pollution

22.A. (1) Where it is apprehended by a Board that emission of any air pollutant, in excess of the standards laid down by the State Board under clause (g) of sub-section (1) of section 17, is likely to occur by reason of any person operating an industrial plant or otherwise in any air pollution control area, the Board may make an application to a court, not inferior to that of a Metropolitan Magistrate or a Judicial Magistrate of the first class for restraining such person from emitting such air pollutant.

(2) On receipt of the application under sub-section *(1)*, the court may make such order as it deems fit.

(3) Where under sub-section (2), the court makes an order restraining any person from discharging or

causing or permitting to be discharged the emission of any air pollutant, it may, in that order, -

(a) direct such person to desist from taking such action as it likely to cause emission;

(b) authorize the Board, if the direction under clause (a) is not complied with by the person to whom such direction is issued, to implement the direction in such manner as may be specified by the court.

(4) All expenses incurred by the Board in implementing the directions of the court under clause (b) of sub-section (3) shall be recoverable from the person concerned as arrears of land revenue or of public demand.

Furnishing of Information to State Board and Other Agencies in Certain Cases

23. (1) Where in any area the emission of any air pollutant into the atmosphere in excess of the standards laid down by the State Board occurs or is apprehended to occur due to accident or other unforeseen act or event, the person in charge of the premises from where which emission occurs or is apprehended to occur shall forthwith intimate the fact of such occurrence or the apprehension of such occurrence to the State Board and to such authorities or agencies as may be prescribed.

(2) On receipt of information with respect to the fact or the apprehension of any occurrence of the nature referred to in sub-section (1), whether through intimation under that sub-section or otherwise, the State Board and the authorities or agencies shall, as early as practicable, cause such remedial measure to be taken as are necessary to mitigate the emission of such air pollutants.

(3) Expenses, if any incurred by the State Board, authority or agency with respect to the remedial measures referred to in sub-section (2) together with interest (at such reasonable rate, as the State Government may, by order, fix) from the date when a demand for the expenses is made until it is paid, may be recovered by that Board, authority or agency from the person concerned, as arrears of land revenue,, or of public demand.

Power of Entry and Inspection

24.(1) Subject to the provisions of this section, any person empowered by a State Board in this behalf shall have a right to enter, at all reasonable times with such assistance as he considers necessary, any place-

(a) for the purpose of performing any of the functions of the State Board entrusted to him:

(b) for the purpose of determining whether and if so in what manner, any such functions are to be performed or whether any provisions of this Act or the rules made thereunder or any notice, order, direction or authorization served, made, given or granted under this Act is being or has been complied with;

(c) for the purpose of examining and testing any control equipment, industrial plant, record, register, document or any other material object or for conducting a search of any place in which he has reason to believe that an offence under this Act or the rules made thereunder has been or is being or is about to be committed and for seizing any such control equipment, industrial plant, record, register, document or other material object if he has reasons to believe that it may furnish evidence of the commission of an offence punishable under this Act or the rules made thereunder.

(2) Every person operating any control equipment or any industrial plant, in an air pollution control area shall be bound to render all assistance to the person empowered by the State Board under sub-section (1) for carrying out the functions under that sub-section and if he fails to do so without any reasonable cause or excuse, he shall be guilty of an offence under this Act

(3) If any person wilfully delays or obstructs any person empowered by the State Board under sub-section (1) in the discharge of his duties, he shall be guilty of an offence under this Act.

2 of 1974

(4) The provisions of the Code of Criminal Procedure, 1973, or, in relation to the State of Jammu and Kashmir, or any area in which that Code is not in force, the provisions of any corresponding law in force in that State or area, shall, so far as may be, apply to any search or seizure under this section as they apply to any search or seizure made under the authority of a warrant issued under section 94 of the said ode or,as the case may be, under the corresponding provisions of the said law.

Power to Obtain Information

25. For the purposes of carrying out the functions entrusted to it, the State Board or any officer empowered by it in this behalf may call for any information (including

information regarding the types of air pollutants emitted into the atmosphere and the level of the emission of such air pollutants) from the occupier or any other person carrying on any industry or operating any control equipment or industrial plant and for the purpose of verifying the correctness of such information, the State Board or such officer shall have the right to inspect the premises where such industry, control equipment or industrial plant is being carried on or operated.

Power to Take Samples of Air or Emission and Procedure to be Followed in Connection Therewith

26. (1) A State Board or any officer empowered by it in this behalf shall have power to take, for the purpose of analysis, samples of air or emission from any chimney, flue or duct or any other outlet in such manner as may be prescribed.

(2) The result of any analysis of a sample of emission taken under sub section (1) shall not be admissible in evidence in any legal proceeding unless the provisions of sub-sections (3) and (4) are complied with.

(3) Subject to the provisions of sub-section (4), when a sample of emission is taken for analysis under subsection (1), the person taking the sample shall-

(a) serve on the occupier or his agent, a notice, then and there, in such, form as may be prescribed, of his intention to have it so analyzed;

(b) in the presence of the occupier or his agent, collect a sample of emission for analysis;

(c) cause the sample to be placed in container or containers which shall be marked and sealed and shall also be signed both by the person taking the sample and the occupier or his agent;

(d) send, without delay, the container to the laboratory established or recognised by the State Board under section 17 or, if a request in that behalf is made by the occupier or his agent when the notice is served on him under clause (a), to the laboratory established or specified under sub-section (1) of section 28.

(4) When a sample of emission is taken for analysis under sub-section (1) and the person taking the sample serves on the occupier or his agent, a notice under clause (a) of sub-section (3), then-

(a) in a case where the occupier of his agent wilfully absents himself, the person taking the sample shall collect the sample of emission for analysist to be placed in a container or containers which shall be marked and sealed and shall also be signed by the person taking the sample, and

(b) in a case where the occupier or his agent is present at the time of taking the sample but refuses to sign the marked and sealed container or containers of the sample of emission as required under clause (c) of subsection (3), the marked and sealed container or containers shall be signed by the person taking the sample, and the container or containers shall be sent without delay by the person taking the sample for analysis to the laboratory established or specified under sub-section (1) of section 28 and such person shall inform the

Government analyst appointed under sub-section (1) of section 29, in writing, about the wilfull absence of the occupier or his agent, or, as the case may be, his refusal to sing the container or containers.

Reports of the Results of Analysis on Samples Taken Under Section 26

27. (1) Where a sample of emission has been sent for analysis to the laboratory established or recognised by the State Board, the Board analyst appointed under sub-section (2) of section 29 shall analyse the sample and submit a report in the prescribed form of such analysis in triplicate to the State Board.

(2) On receipt of the report under sub-section (1), one copy of the report shall be sent by the State Board to the occupier or his agent referred to in section 26, another copy shall be preserved for production before the court in case any legal proceedings are taken against him and the other copy shall be kept by the State Board.

(3) Where a sample has been sent for analysis under clause (d) of sub-section (3) or sub-section (4) of section 26 to any laboratory mentioned therein, the Government analyst referred to in the said subsection (4) shall analyse the sample and submit a report in the prescribed form of the result of the analysis in triplicate to the State Board which shall comply with the provisions of sub-section (2).

(4) Any cost incurred in getting any sample analysed at the request of the occupier or his agent as provided in clause (d) of sub-section (3) of section 26 or when he wilfully absents himself or refuses to sing the marked and sealed container or containers of sample

of emission under sub-section (4) of that section, shall be payable by such occupier or his agent and in case of default the same shall be recoverable from him as arrears of land revenue or of public demand.

State Air Laboratory

28. (2) The State Government may, by notification in the Official Gazette,-

(a) establish one or more State Air Laboratories; or

(b) specify one or more laboratories or institutes as State Air Laboratories to carry out the functions entrusted to the State Air Laboratory under this Act.

(2) The State Government may, after, consultation with the State Board, make rules prescribing-

(a) the functions of the State Air Laboratory;

(b) the procedure for the submission to the said Laboratory of samples of air or emission for analysis or tests, the form of the Laboratory's report thereon and the fees payable in respect of such report;

(c) such other matters as may be necessary or expedient to enable that Laboratory to carry out its functions.

Analysts

29.(1) The State Government may, by notification in the Official Gazette, appoint such persons as it thinks fit and having the prescribed qualifications to be government analysts for the purpose of analysis of samples of air or emission sent for analysis to any laboratory established or specified under sub-section (1) of section 28.

(2) Without prejudice to the provisions of section 14, the State Board may, by notification in the Official Gazette, and with the approval of the State Government, appoint such persons as it thinks fit and having the prescribed qualifications to be Board analysts for the purpose of analysis of samples of air or emission sent for analysis to any laboratory established or recognised under section 17.

Reports of Analysts

30. Any document purporting to be a report signed by a Government analyst or, as the case may be, a State Board analyst may be used as evidence of the facts stated therein in any proceeding under this Act.

Appeals

31. (1) Any person aggrieved by an order made by the State Board under this Act may, within thirty days from the date on which the order is communicated to him, prefer an appeal to such authority (hereinafter referred to as the Appellate Authority) as the State government may think fit to constitute:

Provided that the Appellate Authority may entertain the appeal after the expiry of the said period of thirty days if such authority is satisfied that the appellant was prevented by sufficient cause from filing the appeal in time.

(2) The Appellate Authority shall consist of a single person or three persons as the State Government may think fit to be appoint by the State Government.

(3) The form and the manner in which an appeal may be preferred under sub-section (1), the Appellate Authority shall, after giving the appellant and the

State Board an opportunity of being heard, dispose of the appeal as expeditiously as possible.

Power to Give Directions

31A. Notwithstanding anything contained in any other law, but subject to the provisions of this Act, and to any directions that the Central Government may give in this behalf, a Board may, in the exercise of its powers and performance of its functions under this Act, issue any directions in writing to any person, officer or authority, and such person, officer or authority shall be bound to comply with such directions.

Explanation. For the avoidance of doubts, it is hereby declared that the power to issue directions under this section includes the power to direct-

(a) the closure, prohibition or regulation of any industry, operation or process; or

(b) the stoppage or regulation of supply of electricity, water or any other service.)

CHAPTER V

Fund, Accounts and Audit

Contributions by Central Government

32. The Central Government may, after due appropriation made by Parliament by law in this behalf make in each financial year such contributions to the State Boards as it may think necessary to enable the State Boards as it may think necessary to enable the State Board to perform their functions under this Act:

6 of 1974

Provided that noting in this section shall apply to any [State Board for the Prevention and Control of water Pollution] constituted under section 4 of the Water

(Prevention and Control of Pollution) Act, 1974, which is empowered by that Act to expend money from its fundthereunder also for performing its functions, under any law for the time being in force relating to the prevention, control or abatement of air pollution.

Fund of Board

33. (1) Every State Board shall have its own fund for the purposes of this Act and all sums which may, from time to time, be paid to it by the Central Government and all other receipts (by way of contributions, if any, from the State Government, fees, gifts, grants, donations benefactions or otherwise) of that Board shall be carried to the fund of the Board and all payments by the Board shall be made therefrom.

(2) Every State Board may expend such sums as it thinks fit for performing its functions under this Act and such sums shall be treated as expenditure payable out of the fund of that Board.

6 of 1974

(3) Nothing in this section shall apply to any [State Board for the Prevention and Control of Water Pollution] constituted under section 4 of the Water (Prevention and Control of Pollution) Act, 1974, which is empowered by that Act to expend money from its fund thereunder also for performing its functions under any law for the time being in force relating to the prevention, control or abatement of air pollution.

Borrowing Powers of Board

33A. a board may, with the consent of, or in accordance with the terms of any general or special authority given to it by, the Central Government or, as the case may be, the State Government, borrow money from any source by way of loans or issue of bonds, debentures or such other instruments, as it may deem fit, for discharging all or any of its functions under this Act.]

Budget

34. The Central Board or as the case may be, the State Board shall, during each financial year, prepare, in such form and at such time as may be prescribed, a budget in respect of the financial year next ensuing showing the estimated receipt and expenditure under this Act, and copies thereof shall be forwarded to the Central Government or, as the case may be, the State Government.

Annual Report

35. (1) The Central Board shall, during each financial year, prepare, in such form as may be prescribed, an annual report giving full account of its activities under this Act during the previous financial year and copies thereof shall be forwarded to the Central Government within four months from the last date of the previous financial year and that Government shall cause every such report to be laid before both Houses of Parliament within nine months of the last date of the previous financial year.

(2) Every State Board shall, during each financial year, prepare, in such form as may be prescribed, an annual report giving full account of its activities under this Act during the previous financial year and copies thereof shall be forwarded to the State

Government within four months from the last date of the previous financial year and that Government shall cause every such report to be laid before the State Legislature within a period of nine months from the date of the previous financial year.] Accounts and audit

36. (1) Every Board shall, in relation to its functions under this Act, maintain proper accounts and other relevant records and prepare an annual statement of accounts in such form as may be prescribed by the Central Government or, as the case may be, the State Government.

1 of 1956

(2) The accounts of the Board shall "be audited by an auditor duly qualified to act as an auditor of companies under section 226 of the Companies Act, 1956.

(3) The said auditor shall be appointed by the Central Government or, as the case may be, the State Government on the advice of the Comptroller and Auditor General of India.

(4) Every auditor appointed to audit the accounts of the Board under this Act shall have the right to demand the production of books, accounts, connected vouchers and other documents and papers and to inspect any of the offices of the Board.

(5) Every such auditor shall send a copy of his report together with an audited copy of the accounts to the Central Government or, as the case may be, the State Government.

(6) The Central Government shall, as soon as may be after the receipt of the audit report under sub-section (5), cause the same to be laid before both Houses of Parliament.

(7) The State Government shall, as soon as may be after the receipt of the audit report under sub-section (5), cause the same to be laid before the State Legislature.

CHAPTER VI

Penalties and Procedure

Failure to Comply with the Provisions of Section 21 or Section 22 or with the Directions Issued Under Section 33A

37. (1) Whoever fails to comply with the provisions of section 21 or section 22 or directions issued under section 31A, shall, in respect of each such failure, be punishable with imprisonment for a terms which shall not be less than one year and six months but which may extends to six years with fine, and in case the failure continues, with an additional fine which may extend to five thousand rupees for every day during which such failure continues after the conviction for the first such failure.

(2) If the failure referred to in sub-section (1) continues beyond a period of one year after the date of conviction, the offender shall be punishable with imprisonment for a term which shall not be less than two years but which may extend to seven years and with fine.

Penalties for Certain Acts

38. Whoever-

(a) destroys, pulls down, removes, injures or defaces any pillar, post or stake fixed in the ground or any notice or other matter put up, inscribed or placed, by or under the authority of the Board, or

(b) obstructs any person acting under the orders or directions of the Board from exercising his powers and performing his functions under this Act, or

(c) damages any works or property belonging to the Board, or

(d) fails to furnish to the Board or any officer or other employee of the Board any information required by the Board or such officer or other employee for the purpose of this Act, or

(e) fails to intimate the occurrence of the emission of air-pollutants into the atmosphere in excess of the standards laid down by the State Board or the apprehension of such occurrence, to the State Board and other prescribed authorities or agencies as required under sub-section (1) of section 23, or

(f) in giving any information which he is required to give under this Act, makes a statement which is false in any material particular, or

(g) for the purpose of obtaining any consent under section 21, makes a statement which is false in any material particular.

Shall be punishable with imprisonment for a term which may extend to three months or with fine which may extend to (ten thousand rupees) or with both.

Penalty for Contravention of Certain Provisions of the Act

39. Whoever contravenes any of the provisions of this Act or any order or direction issued thereunder, for which no penalty has been elsewhere provided in this Act, shall be punishable with imprisonment for a term which may extend to three months or with fine which may extend to ten thousand rupees or with both, and in the case, of continuing contravention, with an additional fine which may extend to five thousand, rupees for every day during which such contravention continues after conviction for the first such contravention.

Offences by Companies

40. (1) Where an offence under this Act has been committed

by a company, every person who, at the time the offence was committed, was directly in charge of, and was responsible to, the company for the conduct of the business of the company, as well offence and shall be liable to be proceeded against and punished accordingly:

Provided that nothing contained in this sub-section shall render any such person liable to any punishment provided in this Act, if he proves that the offence was committed without his knowledge or that he exercised all due diligence to prevent the commission of such offence.

(2) Notwithstanding anything contained in sub-section (1), where an offence under this Act has been committed by a company and it is proved that the offence has been committed with the consent or connivance of, or is attributable to any neglect on the part of, any director, manager, secretary or other officer of the company, such director, manager, secretary or other officer shall also be deemed to be guilty of that offence and shall be liable to be proceeded against and punished accordingly.

Explanation.-For the Purpose of this Section-

(a) "company" means any body corporate, and includes a firm or other association of individuals; and

(b) "director," in relation to a firm, means a partner in the firm.

Offences by Government Departments

41.(1) Where an offence under this Act has been committed by any Department of Government, the Head of the Department shall be deemed to be guilty of the offence and shall be liable to be proceeded against and punished accordingly:

Provided that nothing contained in this section shall render such Head of the Department liable to any punishment if he proves that the offence was committed without his knowledge or that he exercised all due diligence to prevent the commission of such offence.

(2) Notwithstanding anything contained in sub-section (1), where an offence under this Act has been committed by a Department of Government and it is proved that the offence has been committed with the consent or connivance of, or is attributable to any neglect on the part of, any officer, other than the Head of the Department, such officer shall also be deemed to be guilty of that offence and shall be liable to be proceeded against and punished accordingly.

Protection of Action Taken in Good Faith

42. No suit, prosecution or other legal proceeding shall lie against the Government or any officer of the Government or any member or any officer or other employee of the Board in respect of anything which is done or intended to be done in good faith in pursuance of this Act or the rules made thereunder.

Cognizance of Offences

43.(1) No court shall take cognizance of any offence under this Act except on a complaint made by-

(a) a Board or any officer authorized in this behalf by it; or

(b) any person who has given notice of not less than sixty days, in the manner prescribed, of the alleged offence and of his intention to make *a* complaint to the Board or officer authorized as aforesaid, and no court inferior to that of a Metropolitan Magistrate or a

Judicial Magistrate of the first class shall try any offence punishable under this Act.

(2) Where a complaint has been made under clause (b) of sub-section (1) the Board shall, on demand by such person, make available the relevant reports in its possession to that person:

Provided that the Board may refuse to make any such report available to such person if the same is, in its opinion, against the public interest.

Members, Officers and Employees of Board to be Public Servants

44. All the members and all officers and other employees of a Board when acting or purporting to act in pursuance of any of the provisions of this Act or the rules made thereunder shall be deemed to be public servant within the meaning of section 21 of the Indian Penal Code (45 of 1860).

Reports and Returns

45. The Central Board shall, in relation to its functions under this Act, furnish to the Central Government, and *a* State Board shall, in relation to its functions under this Act, furnish to the State Government and to the Central Board such reports, returns, statistics, accounts and other information as that Government, or, as the case may be, the Central Board may, from time to rime, require.

Bar of Jurisdiction

46. No civil court shall have jurisdiction to entertain any suit or proceeding in respect of any matter which an Appellate Authority constituted under this Act is empowered by or under this Act to determine, and no injunction shall be granted by any court or other authority in respect of

any action taken or to be taken in pursuance of any power conferred by or under this Act.

Miscellaneous

Power of State Government to Supersede State Board

47. (1) If at any time the State Government is of opinion-

(a) that a State Board constituted under this Act has persistently made default in - the performance of the functions imposed on it by or under this Act, or

(b) that circumstances exist which render it necessary in the public interest so to do, the State Government may, by notification in the Official Gazette, supersede the State Board for such period, not exceeding six months, as may be specified in the notification:

Provided that before issuing a notification under this subsection for the reasons mentioned in clause (a), the State Government shall give a reasonable opportunity to the State Board to show cause why it should not be superseded and shall consider the explanations and objections, if any, of the State Board.

(2) Upon the publication of a notification under sub-section (1) superseding the State Board,-

(a) all the members shall, as from the date of supersession, vacate their offices as such;

(b) all the powers, functions and duties which may, by or under this Act, be exercised, performed or discharged by the State Board shall, until the State Board is reconstituted under sub-section (3), be exercised, performed or discharged by such person or persons as the State Government may direct;

(c) all property owned or controlled by the State Board shall, until the Board is reconstituted under sub-section (3), vest in the State Government.

(3) On the expiration of the period of supersession specified in the notification issued under sub-section (1), the State Government may-

(a) extend the period of supersession for such further term, not exceeding six months, as it may consider necessary; or

(b) reconstitute the State Board by a fresh nomination or appointment as the case may be, and in such case any person who vacated his office under clause (a) of sub-section (2) shall also be eligible for nomination or appointment.

Provided that the State Government may at any time before the expiration of the period of supersession whether originally specified under sub-section (1) or as extended under this sub-section, take action under clause (b) of this sub-section.

Special Provision in the Case of Supersession of the Central Board or the State Boards Constituted Under the Water (Prevention and Control of Pollution) Act, 1974

48. Where the Central Board or any State Board constituted under the Water (Prevention and Control of Pollution) Act, 1974, is superseded by the Central Government or the State Government, as the case may be, under that Act, all the powers, functions and duties of the Central Board or such State Board under this Act shall be

exercised, performed or discharged during the period of such supersession by the person or persons, exercising, performing or discharging the powers, functions and duties of the Central Board or such State Board under the Water (Prevention and Control of Pollution) Act, 1974, during such period.

Dissolution of State Boards Constituted Under the Act

49. (1) As and when the Water (Prevention and Control of Pollution) Act, 1974 (Act 6 of 1974), comes into force in any State and the State Government constitutes a (State Board for the Prevention and Control of Water Pollution) under that Act, the State Board constituted by the State Government under this Act shall stand dissolved and the Board first-mentioned shall exercise the powers and perform the functions of the Board second-mentioned in that State.

(2) On the dissolution of the State Board constituted under this Act,-

(a) all the members shall vacate their offices as such;

(b) all moneys and other property of whatever kind (including the fund of the State Board) owned by, or vested in, the State Board, immediately before such dissolution, shall stand transferred to and vest in the State Board for the Prevention and Control of Water Pollution;

(c) every officer and other employee serving under the State Board immediately before such dissolution shall be transferred to and become an officer or other employee of the

(State Board for the Prevention and Control of Water Pollution) and hold office by the same tenure and at the same remuneration and on the same terms and conditions of service as he would have held the same if the State Board constituted under this Act had not been dissolved and shall continue to do so unless and until such tenure, remuneration and conditions of service are duly altered by the (State Board for the Prevention and Control of Water Pollution):

Provided that the tenure, remuneration and terms and conditions of service of any such officer or other employee shall not be altered to his disadvantage without the previous sanction of the State Government;

(d) ail liabilities obligations of the State Board of whatever kind, immediately before such dissolution, shall be deemed to be the liabilities or obligations, as the case may be, of the State Board for the Prevention and Control of Water Pollution) and any proceeding or cause of action, pending or existing immediately before such dissolution by or against the State Board 'constituted under this Act in relation to such liability or obligation may be continued and enforced by or against the State Board for the Prevention and Control of Water Pollution.

50. (Power to amend the Schedule) Rep, by the Air (Prevention and Control of Pollution) Amendment Act, 1987 (47 of 1987), s. 22 (w.e.f. 1-4-1983).

Maintenance of Register

51. (l) Every State Board shall maintain a register

containing particulars of the persons to whom consent has been granted under section 21, the standard for emission laid down by it in relation to each such consent and such other particulars as may be prescribed.

(2) The register maintained under sub-section (1) shall be open to inspection at all reasonable hours by any person interested in or affected by such standards for emission or by any other person authorized by such person in this behalf.

Effect of Other Laws

52. 'Save as otherwise provided by or under the Atomic Energy Act, 1962 (33 of 1962), in relation to radioactive air pollution the provisions of this Act shall have effect notwithstanding anything inconsistent therewith contained in any enactment other than this Act.

Power of Central Government to Make Rules

53. (1) The Central Government may, in consultation with the Central Board by notification in the Official Gazette, make rules in respect of the following matters namely:-

(a) the intervals and the time and place at which meetings of the Central Board or any committee thereof shall be held and the procedure to be followed at such meetings, including the quorum necessary for the transaction of business thereat, under sub-section (1) of section 10 and under sub-section (2) of section 11;

(b) the fees and allowances to be paid to the members of a committee of the Central Board, not being members of the Board, under subsection (3) of section 11;

(c) the manner in which and the purposes for which persons may be associated with the Central Board under sub-section (1) of section 12;

(d) the fees and allowance to be paid under subsection (3) of section 12 to persons associated with the Central Board under sub-section (1) of section 12;

(e) the functions to be performed by the Central Board under clause (j) of sub-section (2) of section 16;

(f) the form in which and the time within which the budget of the Central Board may be prepared and forwarded to the Central Government under section 34;

(g) the form in which the annual report of the Central Board may be prepared under section 35.

(h) the form in which the accounts of the Central Board may be maintained under sub-section (1) of section 36.

(2) Every rule made by the Central Government under this Act shall be laid, as soon as may be after it is made, before each House of Parliament, while it is in session, for a total period of thirty days which may be comprised in one session or in two or more successive sessions, and if, before the expiry of the session immediately following the session or the successive sessions aforesaid, both Houses agree in making any modification in the rule or both Houses agree that the rule should not be made, the rule shall thereafter have effect only in such modified form or be of no effect, as the case may be; so, however, that any such modification or annulment

shall be without prejudice to the validity of anything previously done under that rule.

Power of State Government to Make Rules

54. (1) Subject to the provisions of sub-section (3), the State Government may, by notification in the Official Gazette, make rules to carry out the purposes of this Act in respect of matter not falling within the purview of section 53.

(2) In particular, and without prejudice to the generality of the foregoing power, such rules may provide for all or any of the following matters, namely:-

(a) the qualifications, knowledge and experience of scientific, engineering or management aspect of pollution control required for appointment as member-secretary of a State Board constitute under the Act;

(a) the terms and conditions of service of the Chairman and other members (other than the member-secretary) of the State Board constituted under this Act under sub-section (7) of section 7;

(b) the intervals and the time and place at which meetings of the State Board or any committee thereof shall be held and the procedure to be followed at such meetings, including the quorum necessary for the transaction of business threat, under sub-section (1) of section 10 and under sub-section (2) of section 11;

(c) The fees and allowances to be paid to the members of a committee of the State Board, not being members of the Board under sub-section (3) of section 11;

(d) the manner in which and the purpose for which persons may be associated with the State Board under sub-section (1) of section 12.

(e) the fees and allowances to be paid under subsection (3) of section 12 to persons associated with the State Board under sub-section (1) of section 12;

(f) the terms and conditions of service of the member secretary of a State Board constituted under this Act under sub-section (1) of section 14;

(g) the powers and duties to be exercised and discharged by the member-secretary of a State Board under sub-section (2) of section 14;

(h) the conditions subject to which a State Board may appoint such officers and other employees as it considers necessary for the efficient performance of its functions under sub-section (3) of section 14;

(i) the conditions subject to which a State Board may appoint a consultant under sub-section (3) of section 14;

(j) the functions to be performed by the State Board under clause (i) of sub-section (1) of section 17;

(k) the manner in which any area or areas may be declared as air pollution control area or areas under sub-section (1) of section 19;

(l) the form of application for the consent of the State Board, the fees payable therefore, the period within which such application shall be made and the particulars it may contain, under sub-section (2) of section 21;

(m) the procedure to be followed in respect of an inquiry under sub-section (3) of section 21;

(n) the authorities or agencies to whom information under sub-section (1) of section 23 shall be to in sub-section (2) other than those referred to (in clause (aa) there of, shall be

(o) the manner in which samples of air or emission may be taken under sub-section (1) of section 26;

(p) the form of the notice referred to in sub-section (3) of section 26;

(q) the form of the report of the State Board analyst under sub-section (1) of section 27;

(r) the form of the report of the Government analyst under sub-section (3) of section 27;

(s) the 'functions of the State Air Laboratory, the procedure for the submission to the said Laboratory of samples of air or emission for analysis or tests, the form of Laboratory's report thereon., the fees payable in respect of such report and other matters as may be necessary or expedient to enable that Laboratory to carry out its functions, under sub-section (2) of section 28;

(t) the qualifications required for Government analysts under sub-section (1) of section 29;

(u) the qualification required for State Board analysts under sub-section (2) of section 29;

(v) the form and the manner in which appeals may be preferred, the fees payable in respect of such appeals and the procedure to be followed by the Appellate Authority in disposing of the appeals under sub-section (3) of section 31;

(w) the form in which and the time within which the budget of the State Board may be prepared and forwarded to the State Government under section 34;

(w) the form in which the annual report of the State Board may be prepared under section 35;

(x) the form in which the accounts of the State Board may be maintained under the sub-section (1) of section 36;

(xx) the manner in which notice of intention to make a complaint shall be given under section 43;

(y) the particulars which the register maintained under section 51 may contain;

(z) any other matter which has to be, or may be, prescribed.

(3) After the first constitution of the State Board, no rule with respect to any of the matters referredto in sub-section (2) other than those referred to (in clause (aa) thereof), shall be made, varied, amended or repealed without consulting that Board.

(The Schedule) Omitted by the Air Prevention and

Control of Pollution) Amendment Act, 1987, S. 28 (w.e.f. 1.4.1983)

THE ENVIRONMENT (PROTECTION) BILL, 1986: A BILL

A bill was passed by Lok Sabha on 8th May, 1986 to provide for the protection and improvement of environment and for matters connected therewith

Whereas decisions were taken at the United Nations Conference on the Human Environment held at Stockholm in June, 1972, in which India participated, to take appropriate steps for the protection and improvement of human environment.

And whereas it is considered necessary further to implement the decisions aforesaid in so far as they relate to the protection and improvement of environment and the prevention of hazards to human beings, other living creatures, plants ad property.

Bill enacted by Parliament in the Thirty-seventh Year of the Republic of India as follows:-

CHAPTER I

Preliminary

1. (a) This Act may be called the Environment (Protection) Act, 1986.

   (b) It extends to the whole of India.

   (c) It shall come into force on such date as the Central Government may by notification in the Official Gazette, appoint and different dates may be appointed for different provisions of this Act and for different areas.

2. In this Act, unless the context otherwise requires,-

   (a) "environment" includes water, air and land and the interrelationship which exists among and between water, air and land, and human beings, other living creatures, plants, micro-organism and property;

   (b) "environmental pollutant" means any solid, liquid or gaseous substance present in such concentration as maybe or tend to be injurious to environment.

   (c) "environmental pollution" means the presence in the environment of any environmental pollutant;

   (d) "handling" in relation to any substance, means the manufacture, processing, treatment, package storage, transportation, use, collection, destruction, conversion, offering for sale, transfer of the like of such substance;

   (e) "hazardous substance" means any substance or preparation which, by reasons of its chemical or physico-chemical properties or handling, is liable to cause harm to human beings, other living creatures, plants micro-organisms, property on the environment;

   (f) "occupier", in relation to any factory or premises, means a person who has control over the affairs of the factory or the premises and includes, in relation to any substance,, the person in possession of the substance;

   (g) "prescribed" means prescribed by rules made under this Act.

CHAPTER II

General Powers of the Central Government

3. (a) Subject to the provisions of this Act, the Central Government shall have the power to take all such measures as it deems necessary or expedient for the purpose of protecting and improving the quality of the environment and preventing, controlling, and abating environmental pollution.

(b) In particular, and without prejudice to the generality of the provisions of Sub-section (2). Such measures may include measures with respect to all or any of the following matters, namely:

(i) co-ordination of actions by the State Governments, officers and other authorities—

(a) under this Act, or the rules made thereunder; or

(b) under any other law for the time being in force which is relatable to the objects of this Act;

(ii) planning and execution of a nation-wide programme for the prevention control and abatement of environmental pollution;

(iii) laying down standards for the quality of environment in its various aspects;

(iv) laying down standards for emission or discharge of environmental pollutants from various sources whatsoever;

Provided that standards for emission or discharge

may be laid down under this clause from different sources having regard to the quality or composition of the emission or discharge of environmental pollutants from such sources;

(v) restriction of areas in which any industries, operations or processes or class of industries, operations or processes shall not be carried out or shall be carried out subject to certain safeguards;

(vi) laying down procedures and safeguards for the prevention of accidents which may cause environmental pollution and remedial measures for such accidents;

(vii) laying down procedures and safeguards for the handling of hazardous substances;

(viii) examination of such manufacturing processes, materials and substances as are likely to cause environmental pollution;

(ix) carrying out and sponsoring investigations and research relating to problems of environmental pollution;

(x) inspection of any premises, plant, equipment machinery, manufacturing or other processes, materials or substances and giving, by order, of such directions to such authorities, officers or persons as it may consider necessary to take steps for the prevention control and abatement of environmental pollution;

(xi) establishment or recognition of environmental laboratories and institutes to carry out the functions entrusted to such environmental

(xii) collection and dissemination of information in respect of matters relating to environmental pollution;

(xiii) preparation of manuals, codes or guides relating to the prevention, control and abatement of environmental pollution;

(xiv) such other matters as the Central Government deems necessary or expedient for the purpose of securing the effective implementation of the provisions of this Act.

(3) The Central Government may, if it considers it necessary or expedient so to do for the purposes of this Act, by order, published in the Official Gazette constitute an authority by such name or names as may be specified in the order for the purpose of exercising and performing such of the powers and functions (including the power to issue directions under Section 5) of the Central Government under this Act and for taking measures with respect to such of the matters referred in sub-section (2) as may be mentioned in the order and subject to the supervision and control of the Central Government and the provisions of such order, such authority or authorities may exercise the powers or perform the functions or take the measures so mentioned in the order as if such authority or authorities had been empowered by this Act to exercise those power or perform those functions or take such measures.

4. (a) Without prejudice to the provisions of Sub-

section (3) of section 3, the Central Government may appoint officers with such designations as it thinks fit for the purposes of the Act and may entrust to them such of the powers and functions under this Act as it may deem fit

(b) The officers appointed under Sub-section (1) shall be subject to the general control and direction of the Central Government or, if so directed by that Government, also of the authority or authorities, if any, constituted under sub-section (3) of section 3 or of any other authority or officer.

(5) Not withstanding anything contained in any law but subject to the provisions of this Act, the Central Government in the exercise of its power and performance of its functions under this Act, may issue directions in writing to any person, officer or any authority and such person, officer, or authority shall be to comply with such directions.

Explanation—For the avoidance of doubts, it is thereby declared that the power to issue directions under this section includes the power to direct,—the closure prohibition or regulation of any industry, operation or the stoppage or regulation of the supply of electricity or water or any other service.

6. (1) The Central government may, by notification in the Official Gazette make rules in respect of all or any of the matters referred to in Section 3,

(2) In particular and without prejudice to the generality of the foregoing power, such rules may provide for nil or any of the following matters namely,

(a) the standards of quality of air, water or soil for various areas and purposes;

(b) the maximum allowable limits of concentration of various environmental pollutants (including noise) for different areas;

(c) the procedures and safeguards for the handling of hazardous substances;

(d) in the prohibition and restrictions on travelling of hazardous substances in different lines;

(e) in the prohibition and restrictions on the location of industries and the carrying on of processes and informations in different areas;

(f) the procedures and safeguards for the prevention accidents which may cause environmental pollution and for providing for medical measures for such accidents.

CHAPTER III

Prevention, Control and Abatement of Environmental Pollution

7. No person carrying on any industry, operation or process shall discharge or emit or permit to be discharged or emitted any environmental pollutant in excess of such standards as may be prescribed.

8. No person shall handle or cause to be handled any hazardous substenance except in accordance with such procedure and after complying with such safeguards as may be prescribed.

9. (1) Where the discharge of any environmental pollutant in excess of the prescribed standards occurs or is apprehended to occur due to any accident or other unforeseen act or event, the person responsible for such discharge and the person in charge of the place at which such discharge occurs or is apprehended to occur shall be bound to prevent or mitigate the environment pollution caused as a result of such discharge and shall also forthwith-

   (a) intimate the fact of such occurrence or apprehension of such occurrence; and

   (b) be found, if called upon, to render all assistance, to such authorities or agencies as may be prescribed.

(2) On receipt of information with respect to the fact or apprehension of any occurrence of the nature referred to in Sub-section (1) whether through intimation under that sub-section or otherwise, the authorities or agencies referred to in sub-section (1) shall, as early as practicable cause such remedial measures to be taken as are necessary to prevent or mitigate the environmental pollution.

(3) The expenses, if any, incurred by any authority or agency with respect to the remedial measures referred to in subsection (2), together with interest (at such reasonable rate as the Government may, by order, fix) from the date when demand for the expenses is made until it is paid may be recovered by such authority or

agency from the person concerned as arrears of land revenue or of public demand.

10\. (1) Subject to the provisions of this section, any person empowered by the Central Government in this behalf shall have a right to enter, at all reasonable times with such assistance as he considers necessary, any place—

(a) for the purpose of performing any of the functions of the Central Government entrusted to him;

(b) for the purpose of determining whether and if so in what manner, any such functions are to be performed or whether any provisions of this Act or the rules made thereunder or any notice, order, direction or authorisation served, made, given or granted under this Act is being or has been complied with;

(c) for the purpose of examining and testing any equipment, industrial plant, record, register, document or any other material object or for conducting a search of any building in which he has reason to believe that an offence under this Act or the rules made thereunder has been or is being or is about to be committed and for seizing any such equipment, industrial plant, record, register, document or other material object if he has reasons to believe that it may furnish evidence of the commission of an offence punishable under this Act or the rules made thereunder or that such seizure is necessary to prevent or mitigate environment pollution.

(2) Every person carrying on any industry, operation or process or handling any hazardous substance shall be bound to render all assistance to the person empowered by the Central Government under sub-section (1) for carrying out the functions under that sub-section and if he fails to do so without any reasonable cause or excuse, he shall be guilty of an offence under this Act.

(3) If any person wilfully delays or obstructs any person empowered by the Central Government under sub-section (1) in the performance of his functions he shall be guilty of an offence under this Act.

(4) The provisions of the Code of Criminal Procedure, 1973 in relation to the State of Jammu and Kashmir or any area in which that Code is not in force. The provisions of any corresponding law in force in that State or area shall so far as may be, apply to any search or seizure under this section as they apply to any search or seizure made under the authority of a warrant issued under Section 94 of the said Code or as the case may be, under the corresponding provision of the said law.

11. (1) The Central Government or any officer empowered by it in this behalf shall have power to take, for the purpose of analysis, samples of air, water, soil or other substance from any factory, premises or other place in such manner as may prescribed.

(2) The result of any analysis of a sample taken

under subsection (1) shall not be admissible in evidence in any legal proceeding unless the provisions of sub-sections (3) and (4) are complete with.

(3) Subject to the provisions of sub-section (4) the person taking the sample under sub-section (1) shall—

(a) serve on the occupier or his agent or person charge of the place a notice then and there in such form as may be prescribed of his intention to have it so analysed;

(b) in the presence of the occupier or his agent person;

(c) cause the sample to be placed in a container or containers which shall be marked and sealed and shall also be signed both by the person taking the sample and the occupier or his agent or other person;

(d) send without delay, the container or the container to the laboratory established or recognised by the Central Government under Section 12.

(4) When a sample is taken for analysis under sub-section (1) and the person taking the sample serves on the occupier or his agent or person, it notice under clause (a) of sub-section (3), then

(a) in a case where the occupier, his agent or person wilfully the sample for analysis to be placed in a container or containers which should be marked and sealed and shall also be signed by the person taking the sample; and

(b) in a case where the occupier or his agent or person present at the time of taking the sample refuses to sign the marked and sealed container containers of the sample as required under clause;

(c) of sub-section (3) the marked and sealed container or containers shall be signed by the person taking the samples, and the container or containers shall be sent without delay by the person taking the sample for analysis to the laboratory established or recognised under section 12 and such person shall inform the Government analyst appointed or recognised under section in writing, about the wilful absence of the person or his agent or person or, as the case may be, refusal to sign the container or containers.

CHAPTER IV

Miscellaneous

18. No suit prosecution or other legal proceeding shall lie against the Government or any officer or other employee of the Government or any authority constituted under this Act or any member, officer or other employee of such authority in respect of anything which is done or intended to be done in good faith in pursuance of this Act or the rules made or orders or directions issued there under.

19. No court shall take cognizance of any offence under this Act except on a complaint made by—

(a) the Central Government or any authority or officer authorised in this behalf by that Government; or

(b) any person who has given notice of not less than sixty-days in the manner prescribed, of the alleged offences and of his intention to make a complaint to the Central Government or the authority or officer authorised as aforesaid.

20. The Central Government may, in relation to its functions under this Act, from time to time require any person, officer, State government or other authority to furnish to it or any prescribed authority or officer any reports, returns, statistics, accounts and other information and such person officer, State Government or other authority shall be bound to do so.

21. All the members of the authority constituted, if any under section 3 and all officers and other employees of such authority when acting or purporting to act in pursuance of any provisions intimation of this Act or the rules made or orders or directions issued thereunder shall be deemed to be public servants within the meaning of section 21 of the Indian Penal Code.

22. No civil court shaft have jurisdiction to entertain any suit or proceeding in respect of anything done, action taken or order or direction issued by the Central Government or any other authority or officer in pursuance of any power conferred by or in relation to its or his functions under this Act.

23. Without prejudice to the provisions of sub-section (3) of section 3 the Central Government may be

Notification in the Official Gazette delegate, subject to such conditions and limitations as may be specified in the notification such of its powers and functions under this Act (except the power to constitute an authority under sub-section (3) of section 3 and to make rules under section 25) as it may deem necessary or expedient to any officer, State government or other authority.

24. (1) Subject to the provisions of sub-section the provisions of this Act and the rules or order made therein shall have effect notwithstanding anything inconsistent therewith contained in an enactment other than this Act.

(2) Where any act or omission constitutes an offence punishable under this Act and also under any other Act then the offender found guilty of such offence shall be liable to be punished under the other Act and not under this Act.

25. (1) The Central Government may, by notification in the Official Gazette, make rules carrying out the purposes of this Act.

(2) In particular, and without prejudice to the generality of the foregoing power, such rules provide for all or any of the following matters namely:—

(a) the standards in excess of which environment pollutants shall not be discharged or emitted, section 7;

(b) the procedure in accordance with and the safeguards in compliance with which hazards substances shall be handled or causes to be under section 8;

(c) the authorities or agencies to which intimation of the fact of occurrence or apprehension of occurrence of the discharge of any environment pollutant in excess of the prescribed standard be given and to whom all assistance shall be liable to be rendered under sub-section (1) of section 11;

(d) the manner in which samples of air or other substance for the purpose of analysis be taken under sub-section (1) of section 11;

(e) the form in which notice of intention to be sample analysed shall be served under clause sub-section (3) of Section 11;

(f) the functions of the environmental laboratory the procedure for the submission to such laboratories of samples of air, water, soil and substances for analysis or test; the form of laboratory report; the fees payable for such report and other matters to enable such laboratories earn,' out their functions under Sub section (1) of section 12;

12. (1) The Central Government may, by notification in the Official Gazette-(a) establish one or more environmental laboratories;

(2) Recognise one or more laboratories to carry out the functions entrusted to an environmental laboratory under this Act.

(3) The Central Government may by notification in Official Gazette, make rules specifying—

(a) the functions of the environmental laboratory;

(b) the procedure for the submission to the said laboratory of samples of air, water, soil or other substance for analysis or tests, the form of the laboratory report thereon and the fees payable for such report;

(c) such other matters as may be necessary or expedient to enable that laboratory to carry out its functions.

13. The Central Government may by notification in the Official Gazette, appoint or recognise such person as it thinks fit and having the prescribed qualifications to be Government Analysts for the purpose of analysis of samples of air water; soil or other substance sent for analysis to any environmental laboratory established or recognised under sub-section (1) of section 12.

14. Any document purporting to be a report signed by a Government Analyst may be used as evidence of the facts stated therein in any proceeding under this Act.

15. (1) Whoever fails to comply with or contravenes any of the provisions of this Act or the rules made or orders or directions issued there under shall in respect of each such failure or contravention be punishable with imprisonment a term which may extend to five years or with in which may extend to one lakh rupees, or with both, and in case

the failure or contravention continues, with additional fine which may extend to live thousand rupees for every day during which such failure or contravention continues after the conviction for the first such failure or contravention.

(2) If the failure or contravention referred to in sub-section (1) continues beyond a period of one year after the date of conviction, the offender shall be punishable with imprisonment for a term which may extend to seven years.

16. (1) Where any offence under this Act has been committed by a company, every person who, at the time the offence was committed, was directly in charge of and was responsible to the company for the conduct of the business of the company as well as the company, shall be deemed to be guilty of the offence and shall be liable to be proceeded against and punished accordingly;

Provided that nothing contained in this sub-section shall render any such person liable to any punishment provided in this Act, if he proves that the offence was committed without his knowledge or that he exercised all due diligence to prevent the commission of such offence.

(2) Not withstanding anything contained in sub-section (1), where an offence under this Act has been committed by a company and it is provided that the offence has been committed with the consent or convenience of or is attributable to any neglect on the part of, any director, manager, secretary or other

officer of the company, such director, manager, secretary or other officer shall also be deemed to be guilty of that offence and shall be liable to be proceeded against and punished accordingly.

Explanation: For the purposes of this section—

(a) 'company' means any body corporate, and include a firm or other association of individuals; and

(b) "director", in relation to a firm, means a partner in the firm.

17. (1) Where an office under this Act has been committed by any Department of Government, the Head of the Department shall be deemed to be guilty of the offence and shall be liable to be proceeded against and punished accordingly;

Provided that nothing contained in this section shall render such Head of the Department liable to any punishment if he proves that the offence was committed without his knowledge or that he exercised all due diligence to prevent the commission of such offence.

(2) Not withstanding anything contained in sub-section (1), where an offence under this Act has been committed by a Department of Government and it is proved that the offence has been committed with the consent or convenience of or is attributable to any neglect on the part of any office other than the Head of the Department, such officer shall also be deemed to be guilty of that offence and shall be liable to be proceeded against and punished accordingly.

(g) the qualifications of Government analyst appointed or recognised for the purpose of analysis of samples of air, water, soil or other substances under Section 13;

(h) the manner in which notice of the offence and of the intention to make a complaint to the Central Government shall be given under clause (b) of section 19;

(i) the authority of officer to whom any reports, returns, statistics, accounts and other information shall be furnished under section 20;

(j) any other matter which is required to be or may be prescribed.

26. Every rule made under this Act shall be laid, as soon as may be, after it is made, before each House of Parliament while it is in session, for a total period of thirty days which may be comprised in one session or in two or more successive sessions, and if, before the expiry of the session immediately following the session or the successive sessions aforesaid, both Houses agree in making any modification in the rule or both Houses agree that the rule should not be made, the rule shall thereafter have effect only in such modified form or be of no effect, as the case may be; so, however, that any such modification or annulment shall be without prejudice to the validity of anything previously done under that rule.

Conclusion

Government of India is taking all necessary precaution and measures legislative, administrative and managerial—

for controlling the fast depletion of environment. Public participation, encouraging awareness and education in people and seeking cooperation both at national and international level are few salient features environmental policy of Government. Recently, the inclusion of Environment Education by U.G.C. in university sylabi and direction given by supreme court of India, shows the Concern of Government.

Bibliography

Allen K. Kneese and Clifford S. Russell (1987). "environmental economics," *The New Palgrave: A Dictionary of Economics*, v. 2, pp. 159–64.

Baumol and Oates (1988) cite a swedish example of a refinery damaging an automanufacturing plant. Negotiation between these parties took place to eliminate the Pareto-relevant externality.

Bell, Simon and Morse, Stephen 2008. *Sustainability Indicators. Measuring the Immeasurable?* 2nd edn. London: Earthscan.

Bishop, R.C., Thomas A.H., and Mary J.K., "Contingent Valuation of Environmental Assets: Comparisons with Simulated market", *N.R.J.,* 23:619 - 633 (1983).

Boulanger, P. M. (2008) "Sustainable development indicators: a scientific challenge, a democratic issue" *S.A.P.I.EN.S.* 1 (1)

Browning. E.E. and Jacquelene M. Browning, "Microeconomic Theory and Applications" (S.P. and Co., 3rd Ed. 189), p. 594.

C. Rangarajan, *Indian Economy-Essays in Money and Finance* (N.D. UBS Publishers, Distributors Ltd., 1988), p. 59.

C.D. Kolstad, *Env. Eco.,* pp. 298-304.

Christiansen, V., "Which commodity tax should supplement the Income Tax?", *J. Public Eco.* 24: 195-220 (1994).

Coase, R.H., "The Coase Theorem and the Empty Core: A Comment," *J. Law Economics,* 24: 183-187 (1981).

Conard, K. and C. Morrison, "The Impact of Pollution Abatement Investment on Productivity change: An Empirical comparison of the U.S., Germany and Canada," *South Econ.* J, 55: 684-697 (1989).

Consultative Group on Sustainable Development Indices. International Institute for Sustainable Development.

Cooter, R.D. "Coase Theorem" in J. Eatwell, M. Milgate, and P. Newman (eds.). *The New Palgrave, A Dictionary of Economics* (Macmillan London, 1987).

Costanza, R., (ed.), *Ecological Economics: The Service and Management of Sustainability,* California University. Press, N.Y. 1991).

Dalal-Clayton, Barry and Sadler, Barry 2009. *Sustainability Appraisal. A Sourcebook and Reference Guide to International Experience.* London: Earthscan.

David Pearce (2002). "An Intellectual History Of Environmental Economics", Annual Review of Energy and the Environment 2002, 27:57–81.

David Pearce, Edward Barbier and Anil Markandya, "Sustainable Development: Ecology and Economic Progress,' (ed.) *Leading Issues in Economic Development* (New York : O.U.P., Seventh Ed., 2000), p. 555.

David W. Pearce and J. Warford, *World Without End: Economics, Environment and Sustainable Development: A Summary* (Washington, D.C., World Bank, 1993), p. 3.

Dean, Judith M & Lovely, Mary E (2008), *Trade Growth, Production Fragmentation, and China's Environment*, Pgs. 3 & 5, National Bureau of

Economic Research, Working Paper 13860, Cambridge, MA

EUROSTAT. (2007). "Measuring progress towards a more sustainable Europe. 2007 monitoring report of the EU sustainable development strategy." Retrieved on 2009-04-14.

Gouler, L.H., I.W.H. Parry, and D. Burtraw (1997), "Revenue Raising Versus Other Approaches to Environmental Protection: The critical Significance of Pre-existing Tax distortions," *Rand J. ECO* 28:708-731.

Hak, T., Moldan, B. & Dahl, A.L. (2007). SCOPE 67. *Sustainability indicators*. Island Press, London.

Hill, J. 1992. *Towards Good Environmental Practice*. The Institute of Business Ethics, London.

Horvath, John Salami Tactics, Telepolis, at Heise.de online, 2000. Retrieved 2009-10-14.

Jean-Marie, Grether & Mathys, Nicole A. & Jaime, de Melo, 2006, *Unraveling the World-Wide Pollution Haven Effect*, Universite de Lausanne, Ecole des HEC, DEEP - Cahiers de Recherches Economiques du Département d'Econometrie et d'Economie politique (DEEP).

Kraus, Christiane (2000), *Import Tariffs as Environmental Policy Instruments*, Springer.

Leonard, Jeffrey H. (1988). *Pollution and the Struggle for the World Product: Multinational Corporations, Environment, and International Comparative Advantage* Pg. 69, Cambridge University Press.

Mani, Muthukumara S. (1966). *Environmental Tariffs on Polluting Imports: An Empirical Study*, , Environmental & Resource Economics, European Association of Environmental and Resource

Economists, Volume 7 Issue 4 (June 1996), pp. 391-411.

Maureen L. Cropper and Wallace E. Oates (1992). "Environmental Economics: A Survey," *Journal of Economic Literature*, 30(2), pp. 675-740.

Meadows, D.H., Meddows, D.L. and Randers, R., '*The Limits to Growth,* 1972.

Michael P. Todaro (2000). *Economic Development* (Reading Masachusetts. Addision-Wesley Longman, Inc.

Parry, I.W.H. (1995). "Pollution Taxes and Revenue Recycling," *J. Envir.Eco.Mgmt.,* 29 (No. 2, Part 2), S: 64 - S-77.

Repetto, R., D. Rothman, P. Faeth and D. Austin (1996). "Has Environmental Protection Really Reduced Productivity Growth," World Resources Institute, Washington, D.C., Oct.

Robert N. Stavins (2008). "environmental economics," *The New Palgrave Dictionary of Economics*, 2nd Edition. Abstract & article.

Robison, David H. (1988). *Industrial Pollution Abatement: The Impact on Balance of Trad*, Canadian Journal of Economics, Canadian Economics Association, Vol. 21, Pgs. 187-99, February.

Schulze, W. and Ralph C. d'Arge (1974). "The Coase Proposition, Information Constraints and Long Run Equilibrium," *Am.Eco. Rev.,* 64:763-772.

Shogren, J.F., Senng, Y.S., Dermot, J.H., and James, B.K. (1994). "Resolving Differences in Willingness to Pay and Willingness to Accept., *A.E.R.,* 84 : 253-270.

Squitres, D. (1992). "Productivity Measurement in Common Property Resource Industries, An Application to the Pacific coast Trawl Fishery," *Rand J. Econ,* 23:221-236.

Singh, M.P. (2004). *Environmental and Pollution,* Anmol, New Delhi.

Stanners, D. et al. (2007). *Frameworks for environmental assessment and indicators at the EEA.* In: Hak, T., Moldan, B. & Dahl, A.L. 2007. SCOPE 67. *Sustainability indicators*. Island Press, London.

Sullivan, C.A. et al. (eds) (2003). The water poverty index: development and application at the community scale. *Natural Resources Forum* 27: 189-199.

W.D. Report (1992). World Bank, pp. 64-65.

Index

T

U

W

■■■